1990s

Ten Years of Popular Hits Arranged for EASY PIANO

Arranged by Dan Coates

Contents

Amazed 4

Beautiful Stranger 8

Beauty and the Beast (from Walt Disney's *Beauty and the Beast*) 14

Because You Loved Me 101

Breakfast at Tiffany's 18

Can You Feel the Love Tonight (from Walt Disney's *The Lion King*) 22

Colors of the Wind (from Walt Disney's *Pocahontas*) 25

Get Here 30

Heal the World 34

Hero 38

How Do I Live 41

I Don't Want to Miss a Thing 46

I Have Nothing 62

I Knew I Loved You 50

I Love You Always Forever 54

I Swear 58

I'll Be There for You (Theme from *Friends*) 67

Livin' la Vida Loca 72

Love Is 78

Love Will Lead You Back 83

Macarena 88

One of Us 92

The Prayer 96

The River 106

Smooth 110

Thank You 120

This Kiss 114

Un-Break My Heart 123

Valentine 128

Walkin' on the Sun 132

A Whole New World (from Walt Disney's *Aladdin*) 137

You've Got a Friend in Me (from *Toy Story*) 140

4

AMAZED

The country-pop band Lonestar was formed in 1992 in Nashville and has been extremely successful with nine #1 singles on the Billboard Hot Country Songs chart. Their signature song "Amazed" was released in 1999 and spent eight weeks at #1. A remixed version of the song spent two weeks at #1 on the pop charts.

Words and Music by
Marv Green, Aimee Mayo, and Chris Lindsey
Arranged by Dan Coates

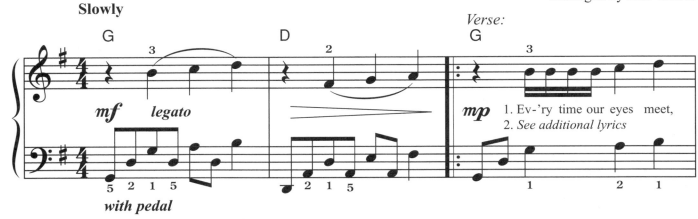

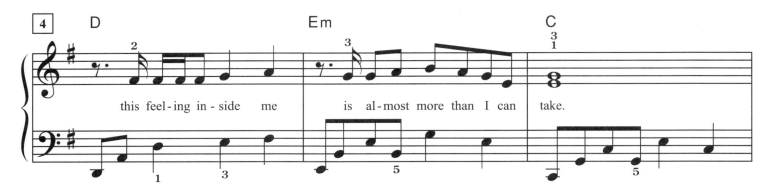

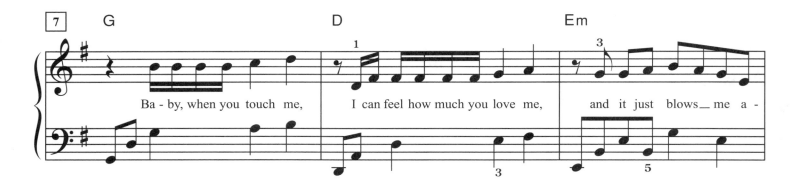

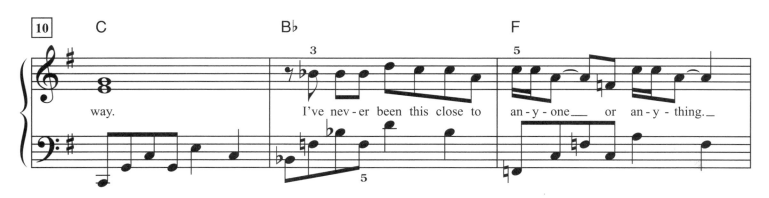

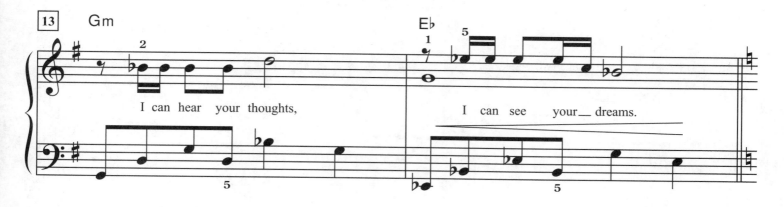

Chorus:

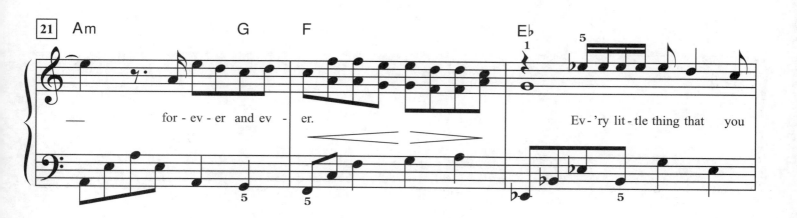

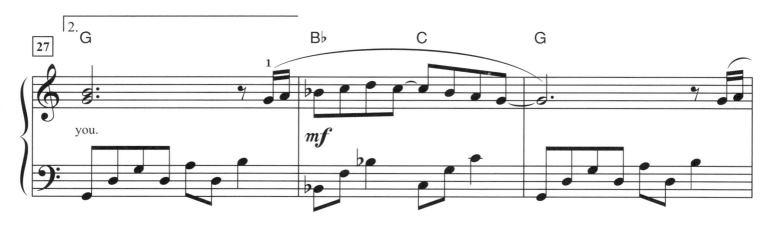

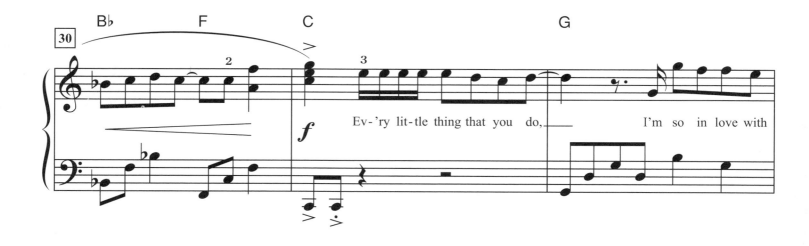

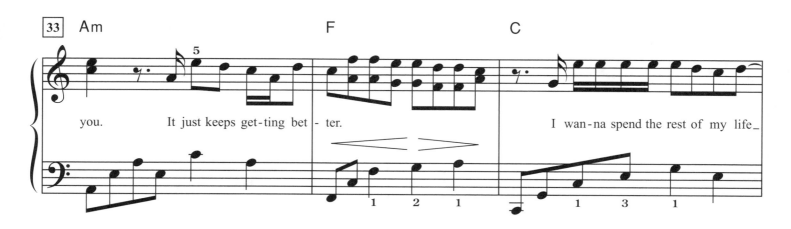

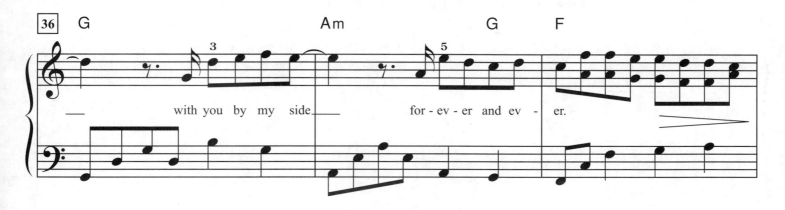

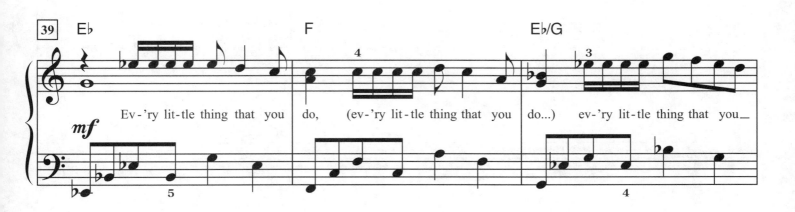

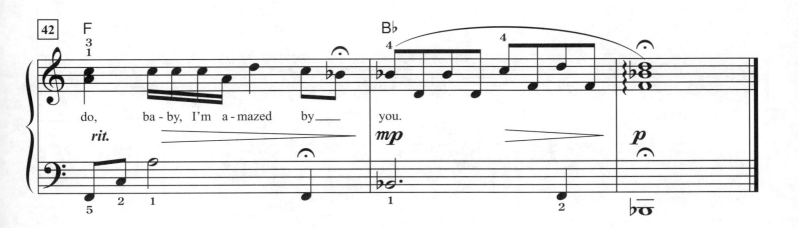

Verse 2:
The smell of your skin,
The taste of your kiss,
The way you whisper in the dark.
Your hair all around me,
Baby, you surround me.
You touch every place in my heart.
Oh, it feels like the first time every time.
I wanna spend the whole night in your eyes.
(To Chorus:)

BEAUTIFUL STRANGER

In 1999 Madonna co-wrote "Beautiful Stranger" with William Orbit (who also worked with Madonna on her *Ray of Light* album) for *Austin Powers: The Spy Who Shagged Me,* the second film in the *Austin Powers* series. The song was never released as a single but received a substantial amount of radio airplay leading to a #19 position on the Billboard Hot 100 and over $2 million soundtrack sales.

Words and Music by
Madonna Ciccone and William Orbit
Arranged by Dan Coates

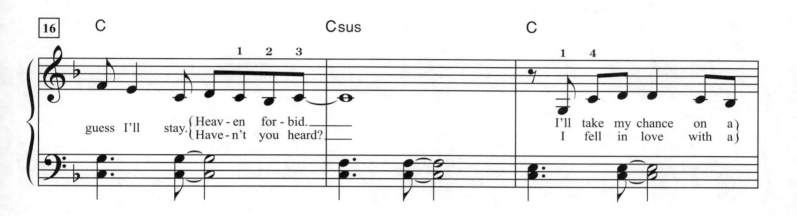

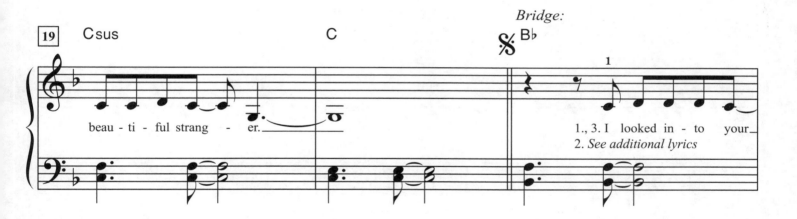

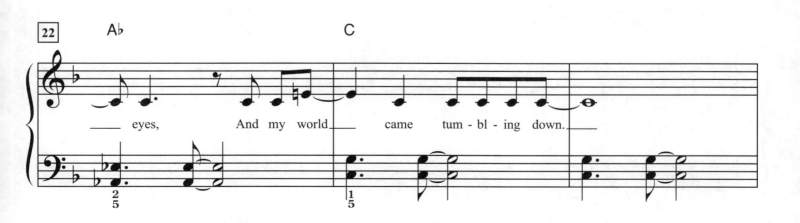

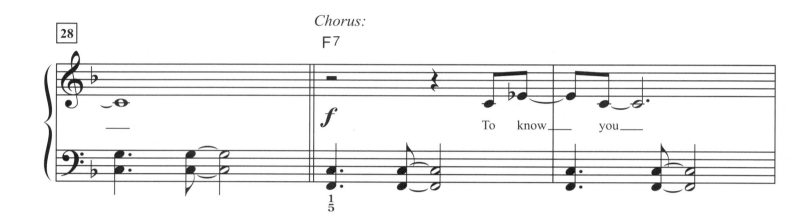

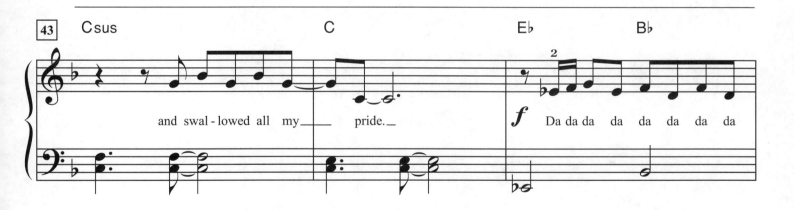

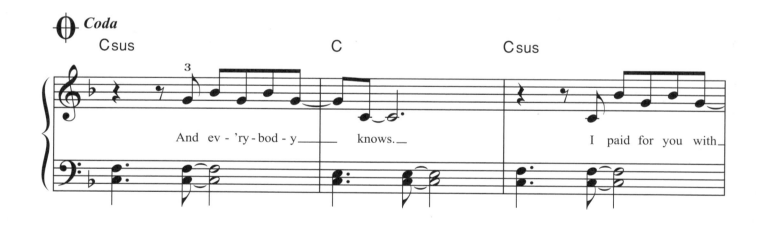

Bridge 2:
I looked into your face,
My heart was dancin' all over the place.
I'd like to change my point of view,
If I could just forget about you.
(To Chorus:)

BEAUTY AND THE BEAST
(from Walt Disney's *Beauty and the Beast*)

In 1991 Walt Disney Pictures released *Beauty and the Beast*, an animated feature film based on the well-known fairy tale. It is the first and only animated film to be nominated for a Best Picture Academy Award. "Beauty and the Beast" is the leading single from the film and was sung in the movie by Angela Lansbury (as Mrs. Potts, the enchanted tea pot). Over the closing credits, Céline Dion and Peabo Bryson performed the song as a duet.

Music by Alan Menken
Lyrics by Howard Ashman
Arranged by Dan Coates

Slowly, with expression

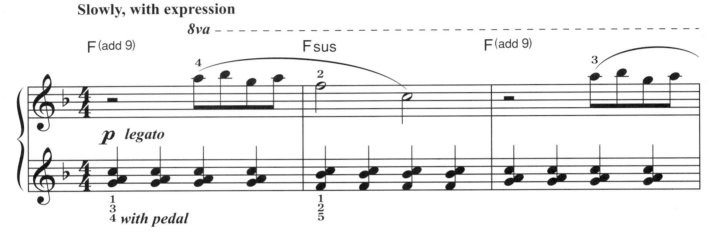

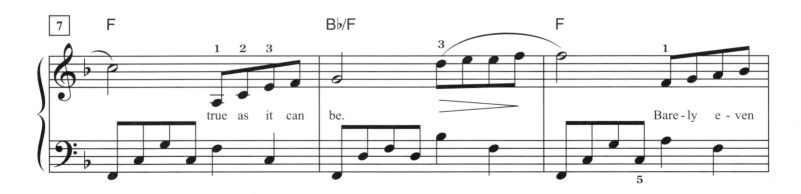

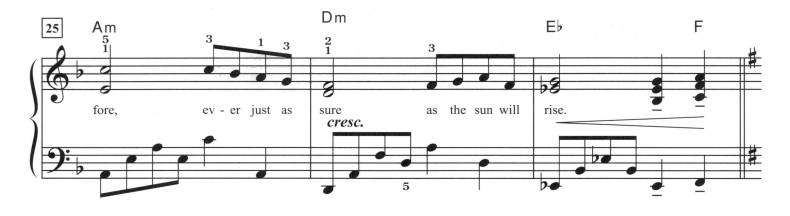

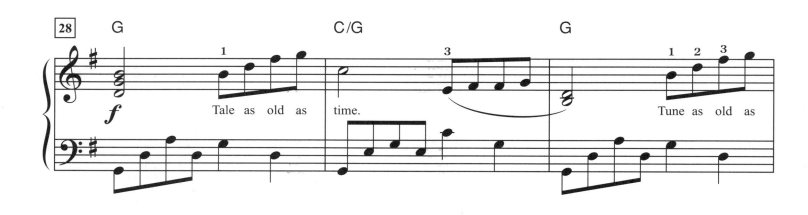

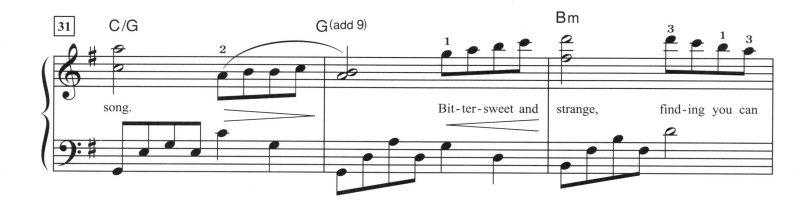

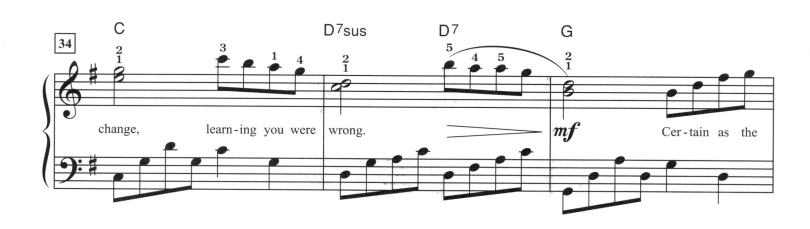

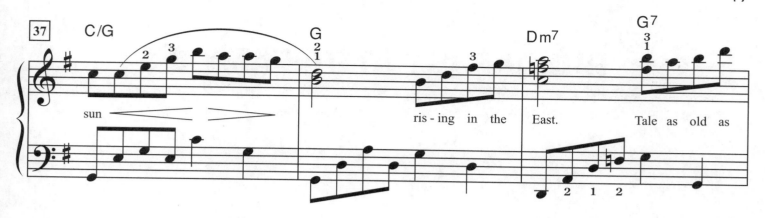

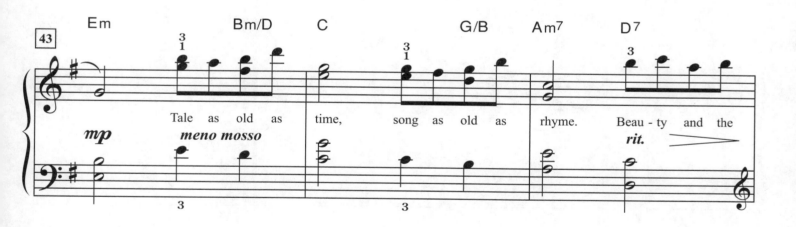

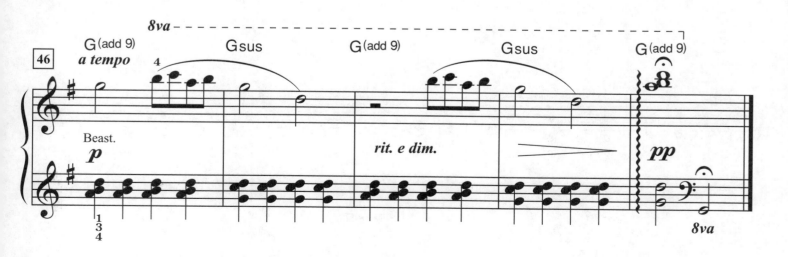

BREAKFAST AT TIFFANY'S

The alternative rock band Deep Blue Something was formed in 1993 in Denton, Texas. The title of their biggest hit, "Breakfast at Tiffany's" (1995), comes from the 1961 Audrey Hepburn movie of the same name. The song reached #5 in the United States and #1 in the U.K.

Words and Music by Todd Pipes
Arranged by Dan Coates

Moderately, with a steady rock beat

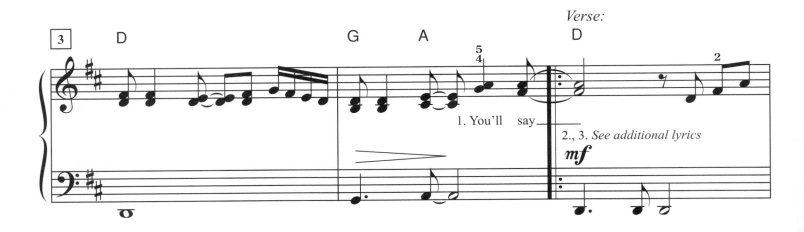

1. You'll say

2., 3. *See additional lyrics*

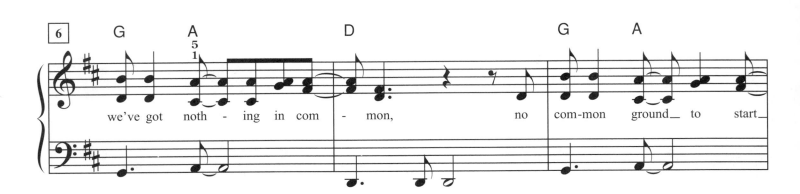

we've got noth-ing in com - mon, no com-mon ground to start

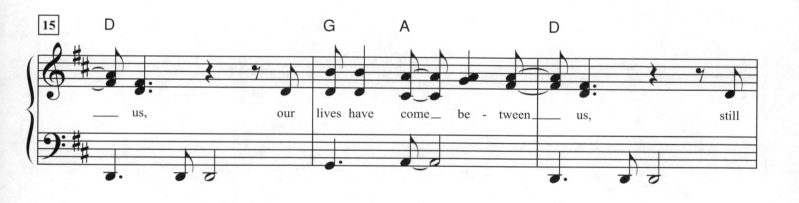

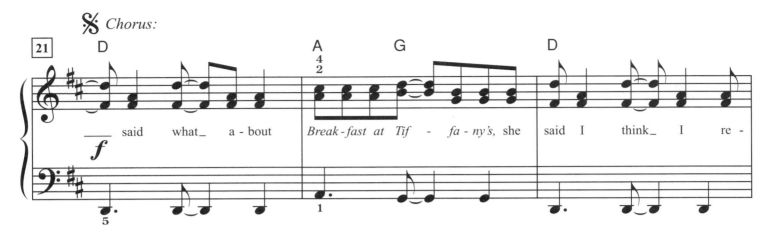

𝄋 *Chorus:*

21 D ... A G D

said what_ a-bout *Break-fast at Tif - fa-ny's,* she said I think_ I re-

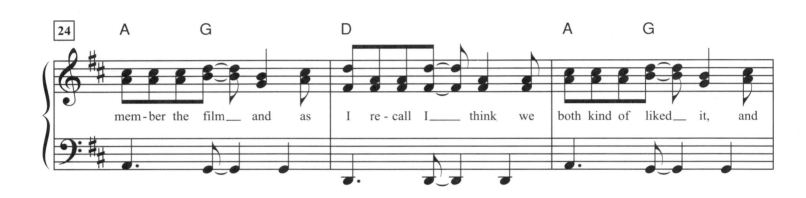

24 A G D A G

mem-ber the film_ and as I re-call I___ think we both kind of liked_ it, and

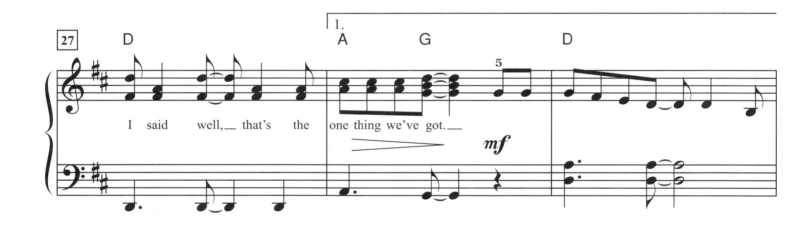

27 D A G D

I said well,_ that's the one thing we've got._

mf

1.

30 G A D G A

2. I see_

21

Verse 2:
I see you, the only one who knew me,
But now your eyes see through me.
I guess I was wrong.
So what now?
It's plain to see we're over,
I hate when things are over,
When so much is left undone.
(To Chorus:)

Verse 3:
You'll say we've got nothing in common,
No common ground to start from,
And we're falling apart.
You'll say
The world has come between us,
Our lives have come between us,
Still I know you just don't care.
(To Chorus:)

Can You Feel the Love Tonight
(from Walt Disney's *The Lion King*)

The Lion King (1994) is Walt Disney's 32nd animated feature film and one of the highest-grossing animated films in history. The film won two Academy Awards: Best Original Score (Hans Zimmer) and Best Original Song for "Can You Feel the Love Tonight" (Elton John and Tim Rice). Elton John performed "Can You Feel the Love Tonight" for the closing credits of the film and won a Grammy Award for the performance.

Music by Elton John
Words by Tim Rice
Arranged by Dan Coates

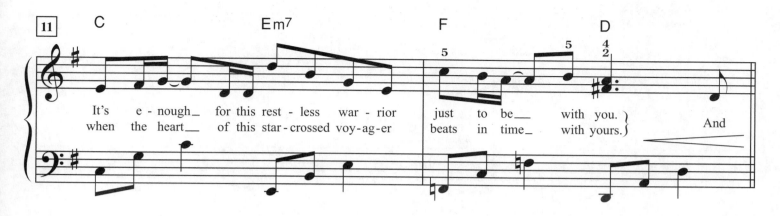

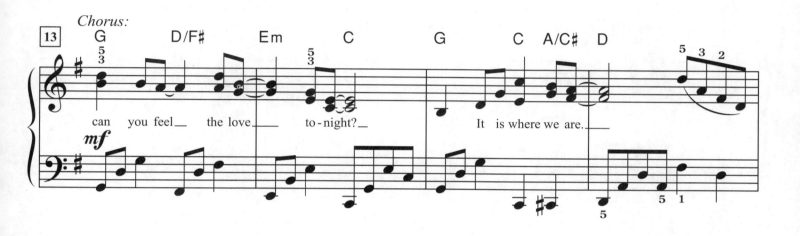

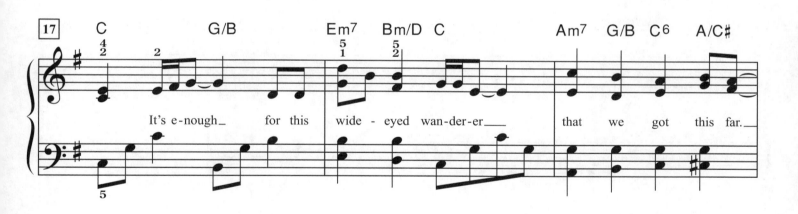

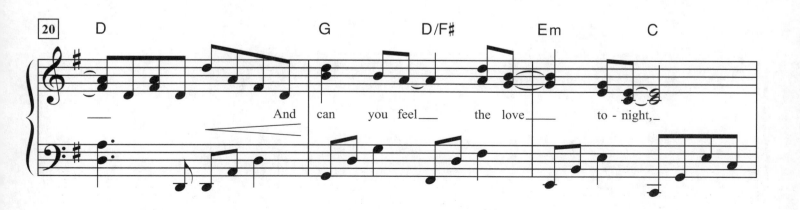

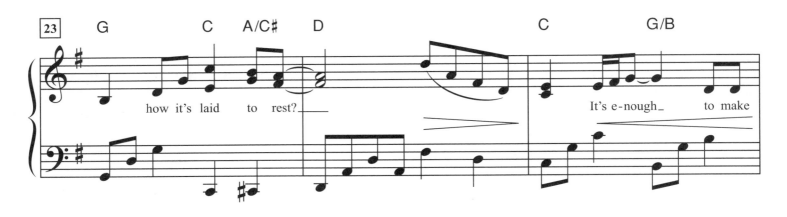

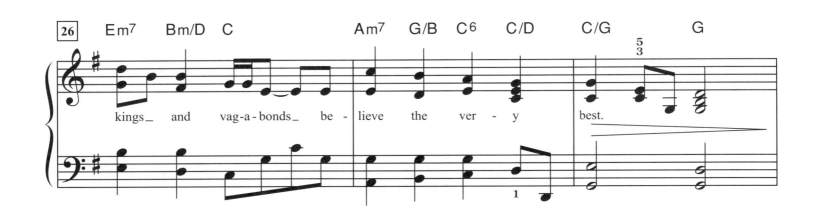

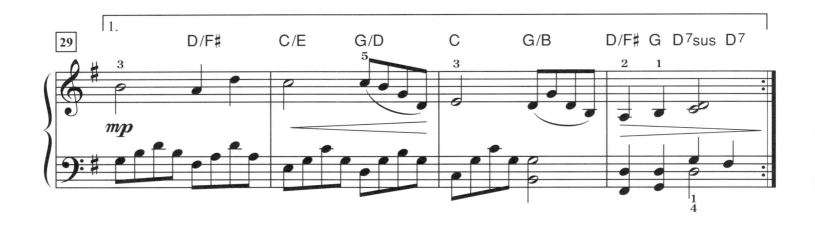

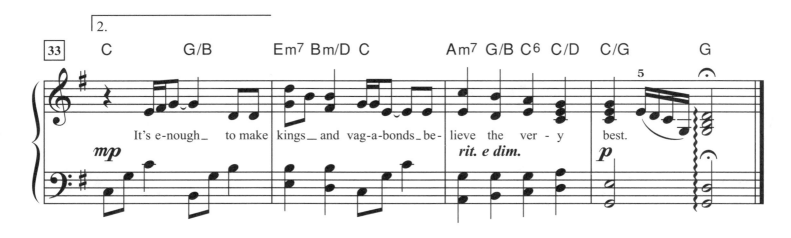

COLORS OF THE WIND
(from Walt Disney's *Pocahontas*)

"Colors of the Wind" is the Oscar-winning Best Original Song from Walt Disney's *Pocahontas* (1995). In the film, Pocahontas (as sung by Judy Kuhn), the beautiful Native American princess, sings this song to convince British explorer John Smith of the wisdom of her people—of mankind's connection to nature. Vanessa Williams recorded the song for the end credits. Released as a single, the song reached #4 on the Billboard Hot 100, and the movie's soundtrack reached #1 on the Billboard 200.

Lyrics by Stephen Schwartz
Music by Alan Menken
Arranged by Dan Coates

Moderately slow

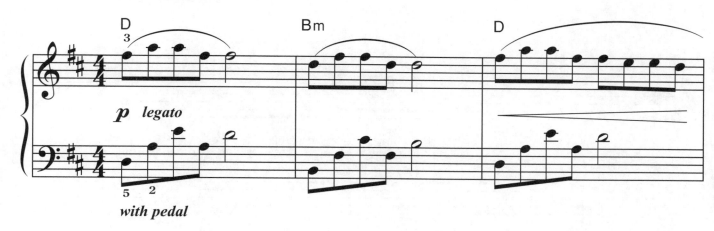

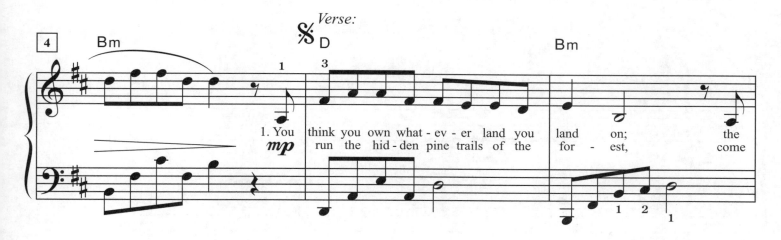

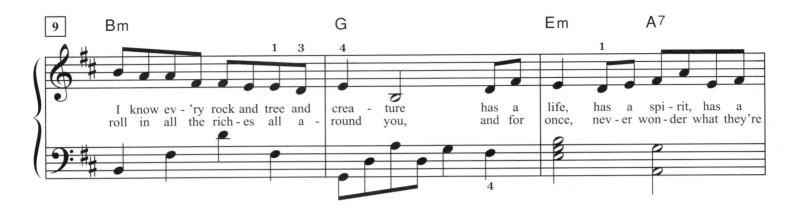

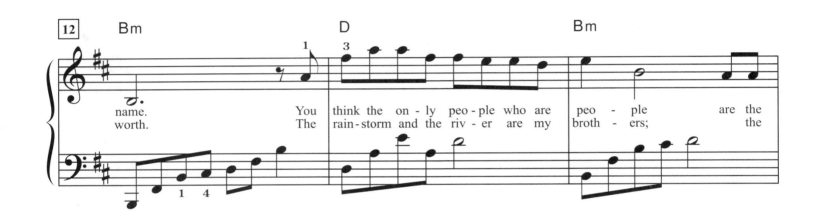

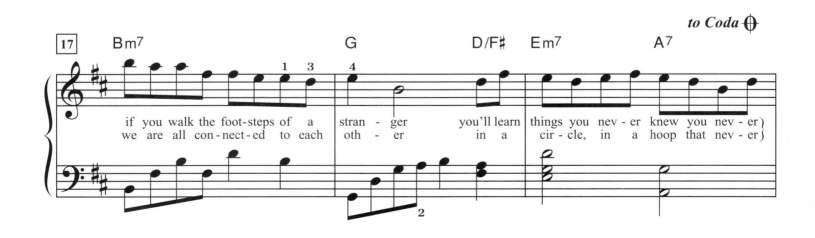

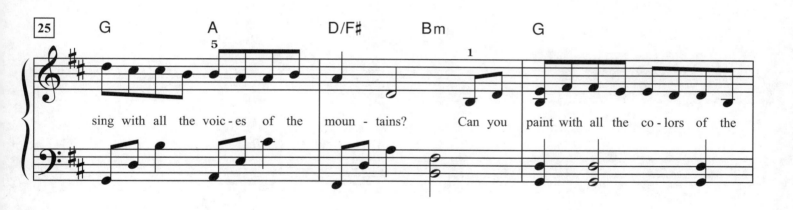

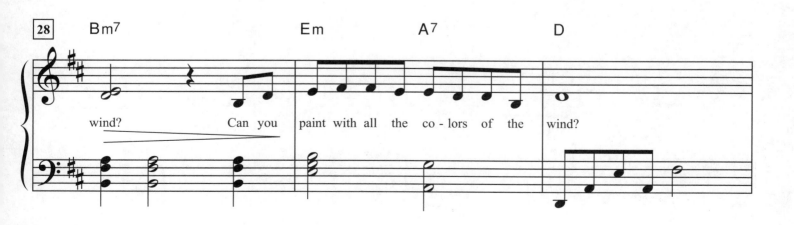

28

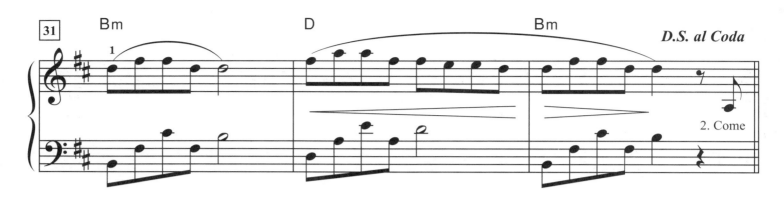

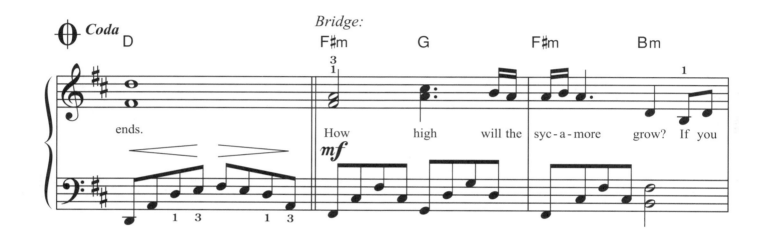

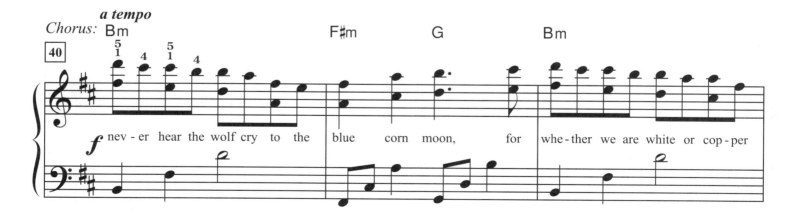

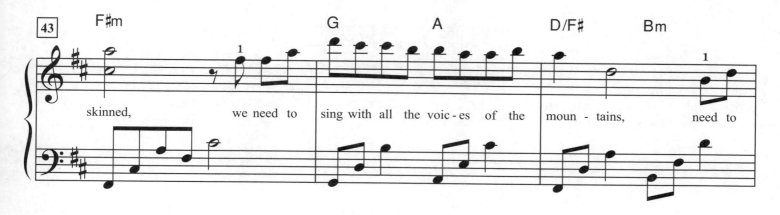

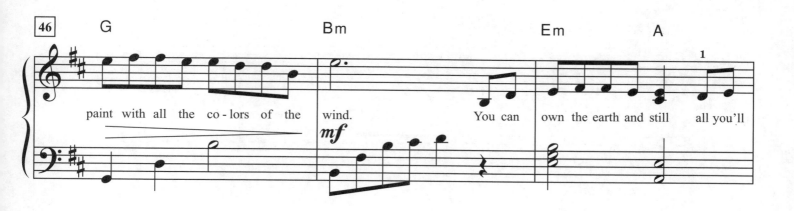

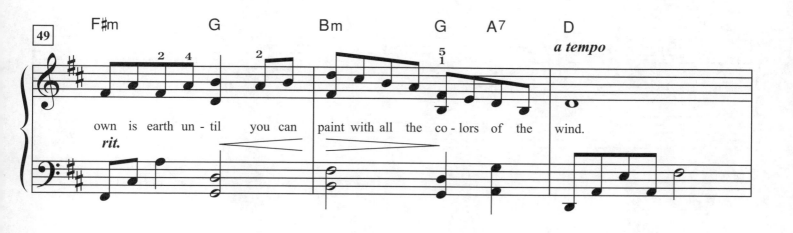

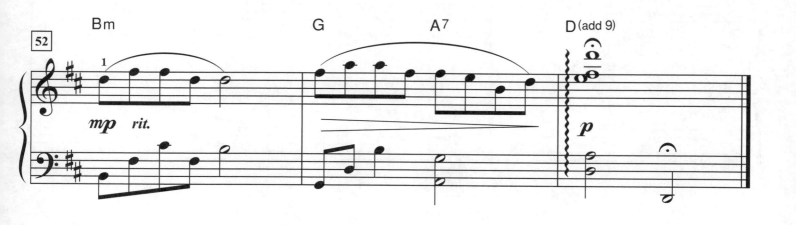

GET HERE

In 1988 singer-songwriter Brenda Russell released her album *Get Here* which garnered her three Grammy nominations. In 1991 the title track was covered by soul, jazz, and gospel singer, Oleta Adams, on her album *Circle of One* which was co-produced by Roland Orzabal (from the British band Tears for Fears) and Dave Bascombe. "Get Here" is Adams's biggest hit and reached the top of the charts in both the United States and the U.K.

Words and Music by Brenda Russell
Arranged by Dan Coates

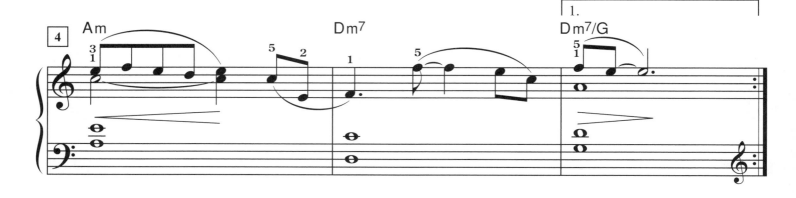

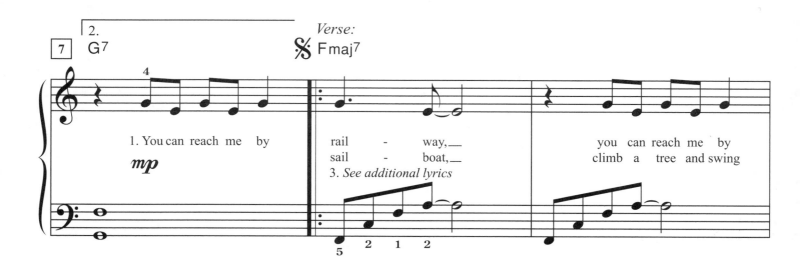

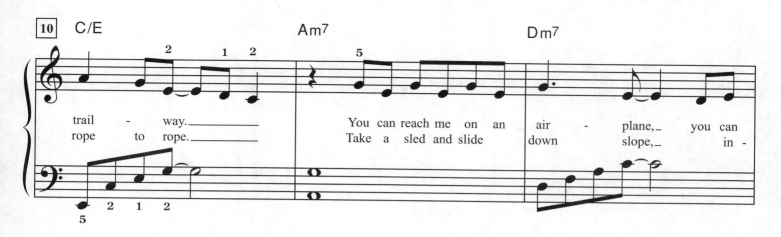

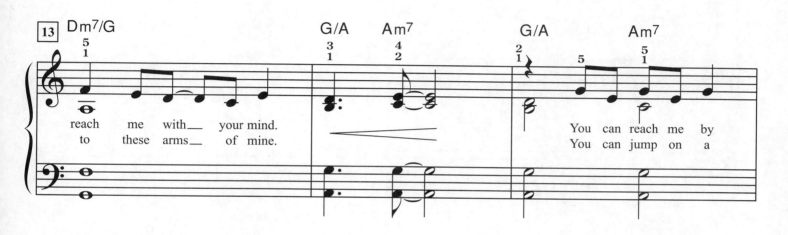

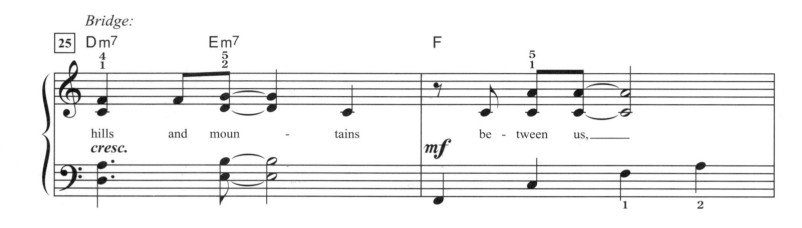

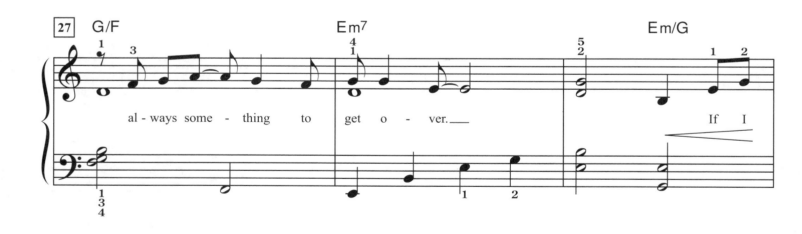

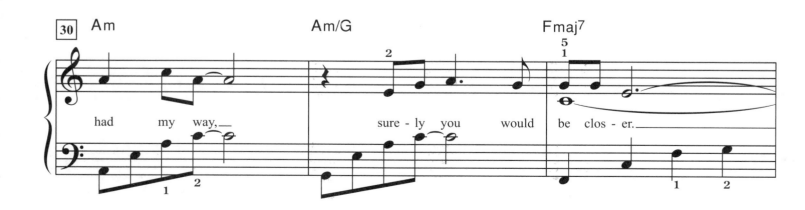

Verse 3:
You can windsurf into my life,
Take me up on a carpet ride.
You can make it in a big balloon,
But you better make it soon.

You can reach me by caravan,
Cross the desert like an Arab man.
I don't care how you get here,
Just get here if you can.

HEAL THE WORLD

"Heal the World" was first released in 1991 on Michael Jackson's album *Dangerous*. Between 1992 and 1993 Jackson performed around the world on his Dangerous World Tour of which all proceeds went to his Heal the World Foundation, a charity he established in 1992. Jackson also performed "Heal the World" during the halftime show at Super Bowl XXVII, one of the most-watched television events in history.

Written and Composed by Michael Jackson
Arranged by Dan Coates

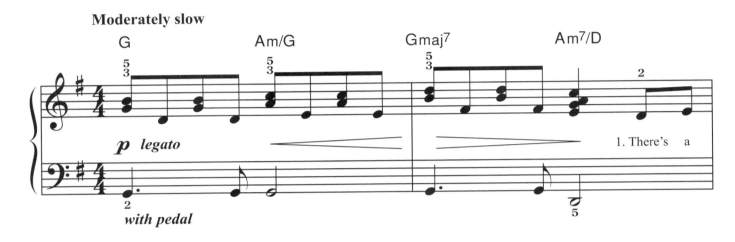

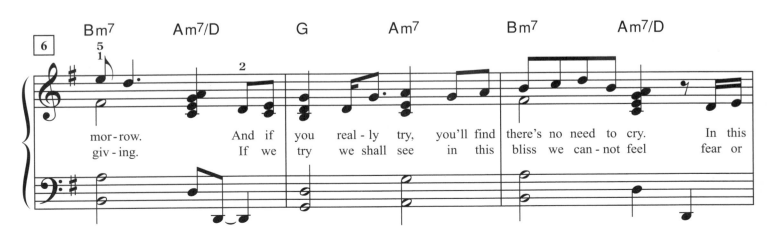

35

36

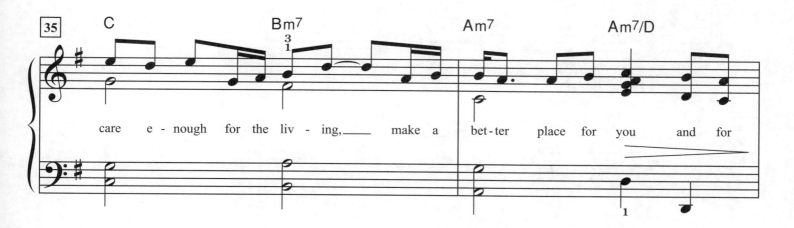

Verse 3:
We could fly so high,
Let our spirits never die.
In my heart, I feel you are all my brothers.
Create a world with no fear,
Together we cry happy tears.
See the nation turn their swords into plowshares.
We could really get there,
If you cared enough for the living.
Make a little space
To make a better place.
(To Chorus:)

HERO

"Hero" is one of the singles from Mariah Carey's most successful album *Music Box* (1993). Carey co-wrote the song with Walter Afanasieff for the Dustin Hoffman film *Hero* (1992), but it was replaced with "Heart of a Hero" sung by Luther Vandross. As a single, the song was a great success for Carey, becoming her eighth #1 single on the Billboard Hot 100 and selling over 3 million copies worldwide.

Words and Music by
Walter Afanasieff and Mariah Carey
Arranged by Dan Coates

HOW DO I LIVE

LeAnn Rimes and Trisha Yearwood both released successful versions of "How Do I Live" in 1997. Rimes's single spent a record 69 weeks on the Billboard Hot 100, and Yearwood won a Grammy Award for her version. The song was originally commissioned by the producers of the 1997 blockbuster *Con Air*. Because it had a more country than pop sound, Yearwood's version was chosen for the film.

Words and Music by Diane Warren
Arranged by Dan Coates

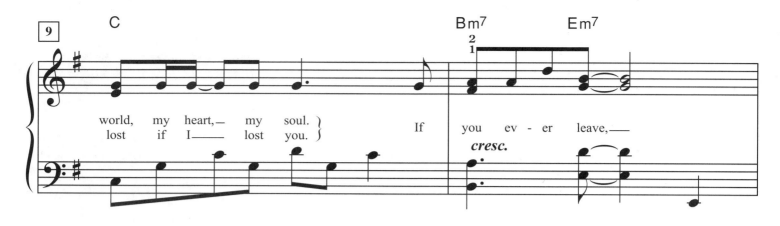

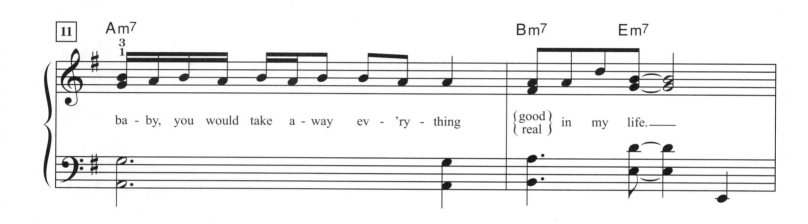

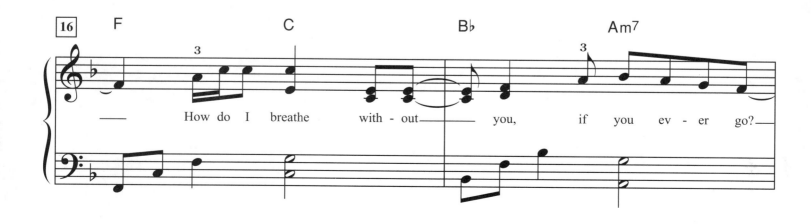

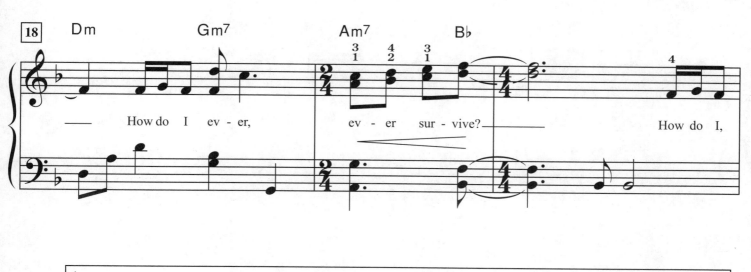

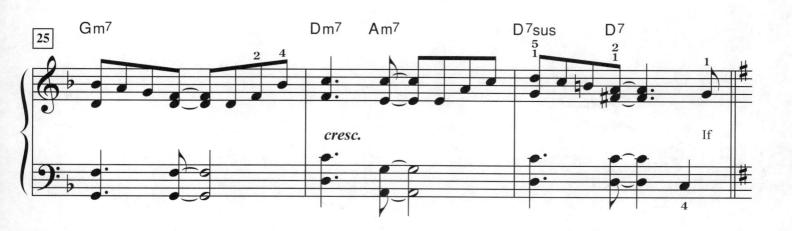

44

Bridge:

you ev - er leave,—— ba - by, you would take a - way ev - 'ry - thing.

Need you with me.—— Ba - by, 'cause you know that you're ev - 'ry - thing

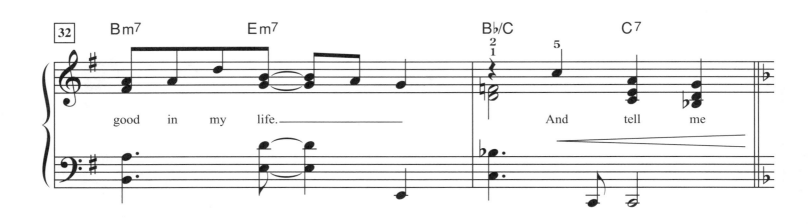

good in my life.———————— And tell me

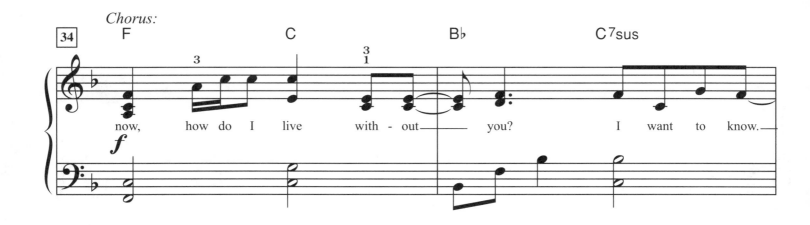

Chorus:

now, how do I live with - out—— you? I want to know.——

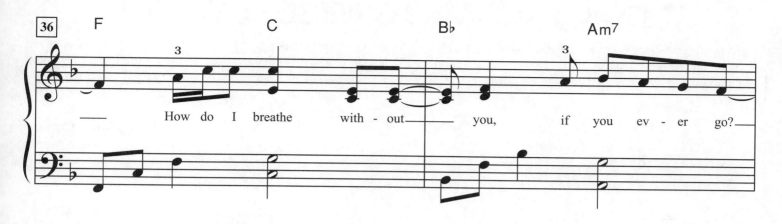

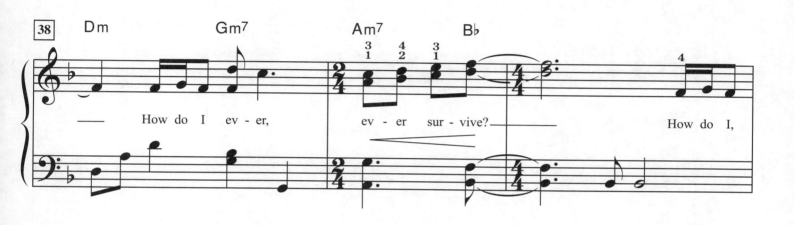

I DON'T WANT TO MISS A THING

Aerosmith recorded the power ballad "I Don't Want to Miss a Thing" in 1998 for the sci-fi blockbuster *Armageddon*. The single debuted on the Billboard Hot 100 at #1, was nominated for an Academy Award, and introduced the band to a new generation of listeners.

Words and Music by Diane Warren
Arranged by Dan Coates

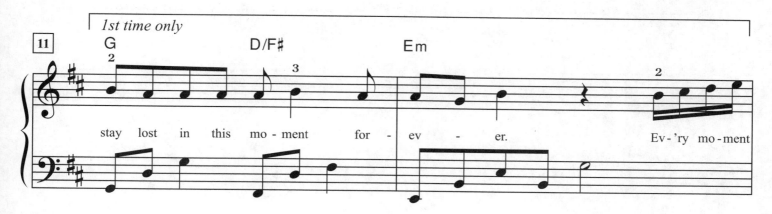

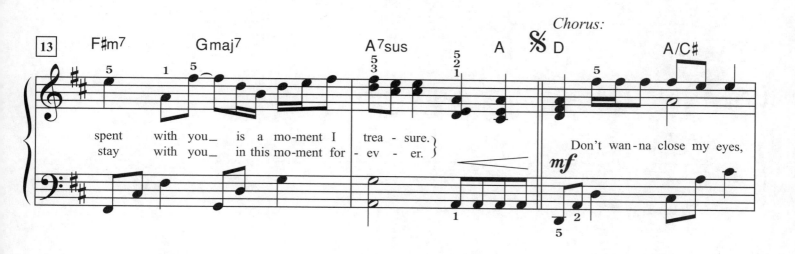

48

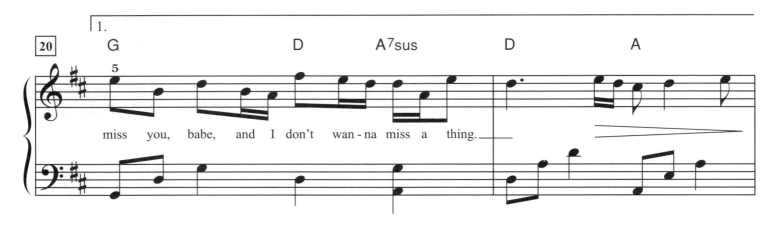

Bridge:

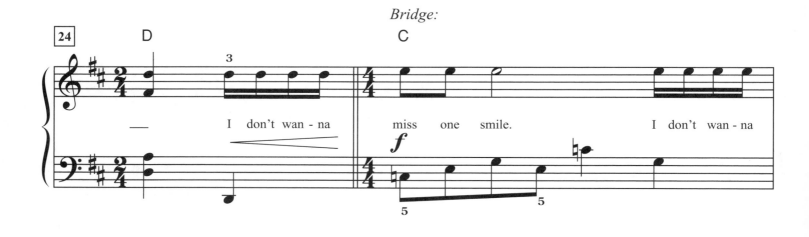

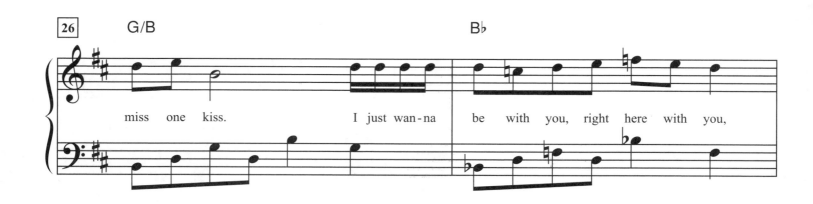

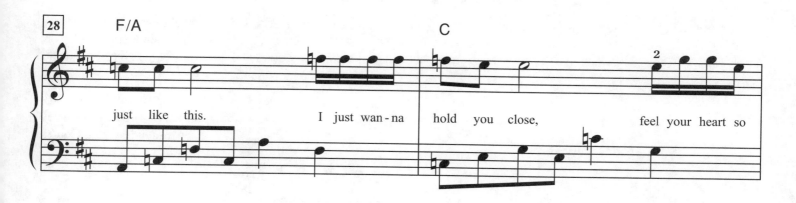

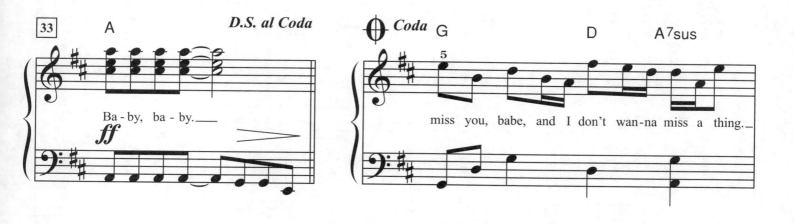

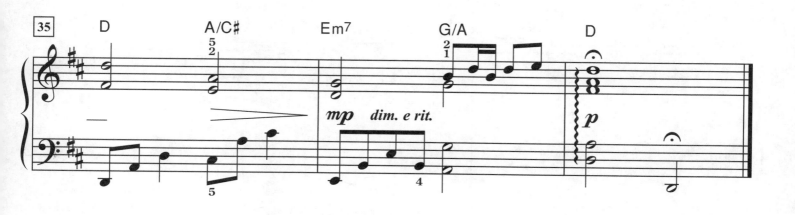

I KNEW I LOVED YOU

The Australian pop duo Savage Garden was one of the most successful bands in the '90s, selling over 23 million albums worldwide. "I Knew I Loved You" is from their 1999 album *Affirmation* and is their second #1 hit after their signature song "Truly Madly Deeply." The music video for "I Knew I Loved You" takes place in a subway station and features actress Kirsten Dunst.

Words and Music by
Darren Hayes and Danie Jones
Arranged by Dan Coates

52

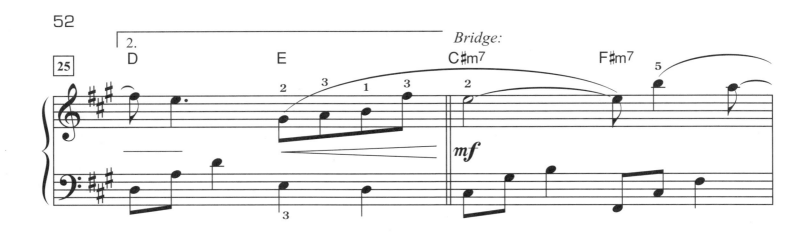

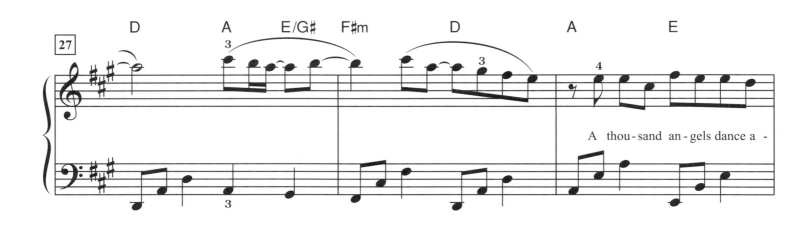

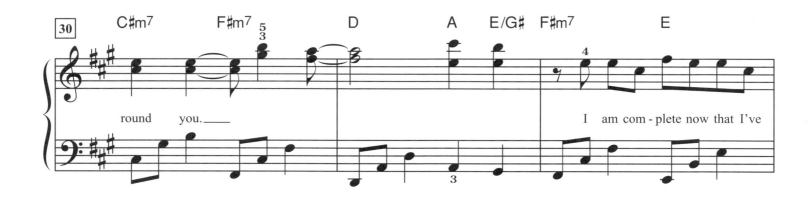

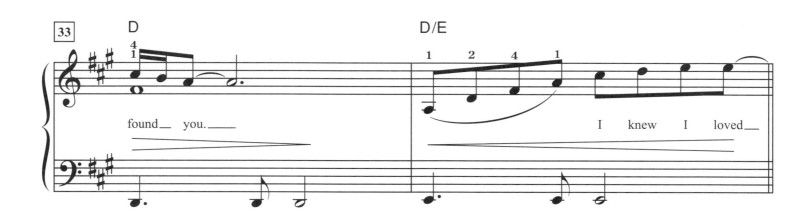

Chorus:

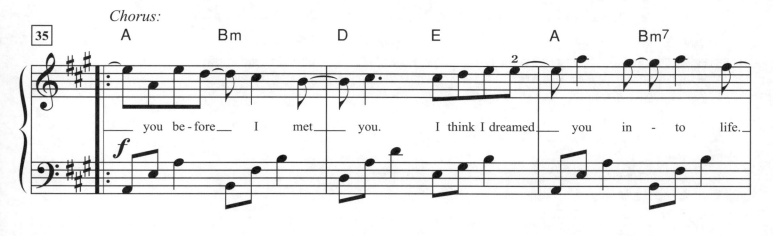

you be-fore___ I met___ you. I think I dreamed___ you in - to life.___

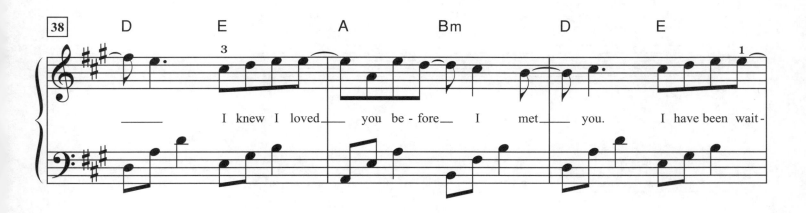

___ I knew I loved___ you be-fore___ I met___ you. I have been wait-

ing all___ my life.___ I knew I loved___ ___ you.

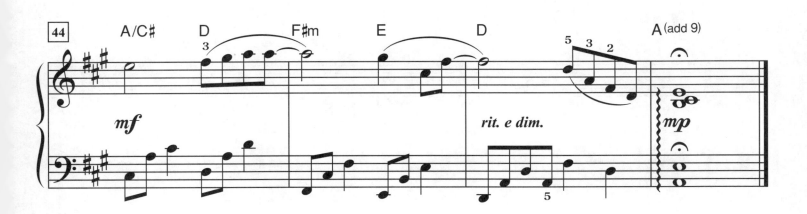

rit. e dim.

I LOVE YOU ALWAYS FOREVER

Welsh singer-songwriter Donna Lewis released her debut album *Now in a Minute* in 1996. "I Love You Always Forever" was the incredibly successful single from that album, becoming one of the most-played songs of the '90s. According to Lewis, the song was inspired by *Love for Lydia,* a 1952 novel written by British author H. E. Bates.

Words and Music by Donna Lewis
Arranged by Dan Coates

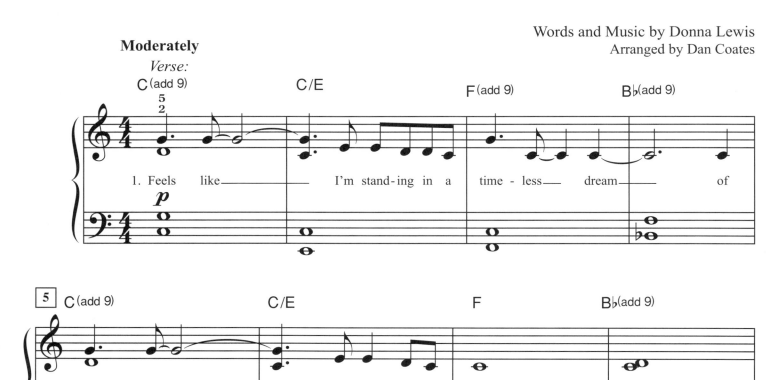

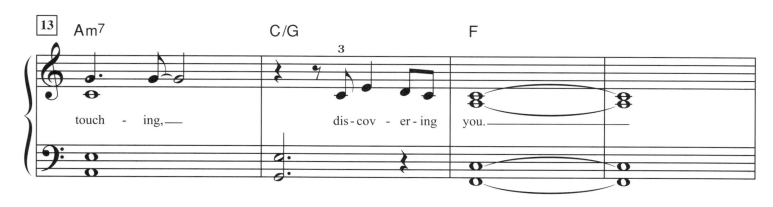

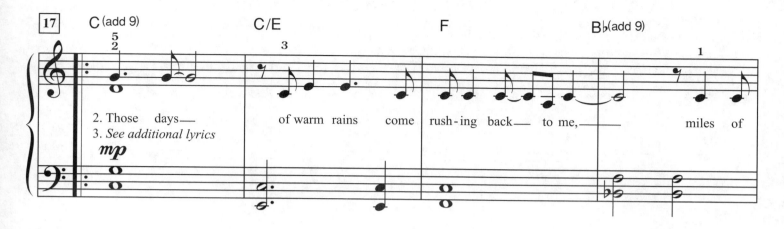

2. Those days— of warm rains come rush-ing back— to me,— miles of
3. *See additional lyrics*
mp

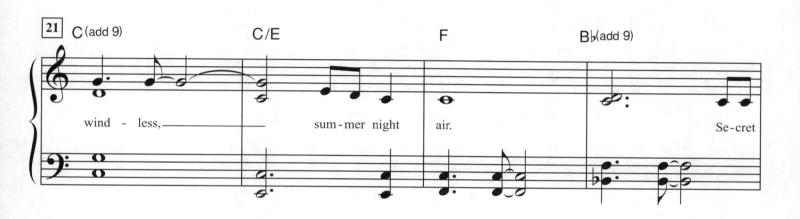

wind - less,——————— sum-mer night air. Se-cret

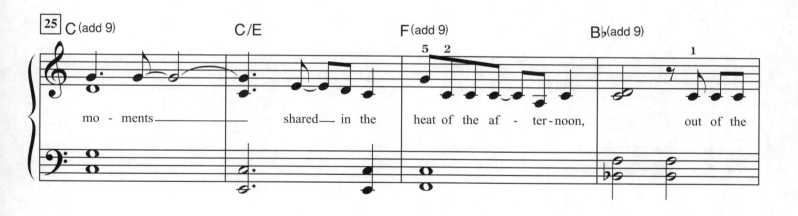

mo - ments——————— shared— in the heat of the af - ter-noon, out of the

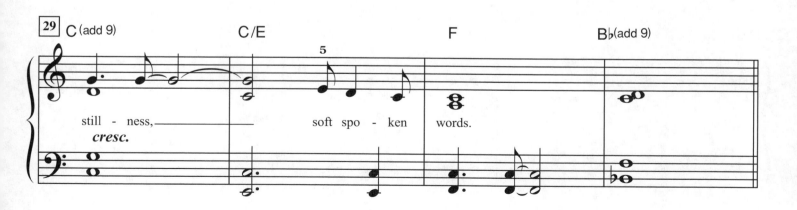

still - ness,——————— soft spo - ken words.
cresc.

56

Chorus:

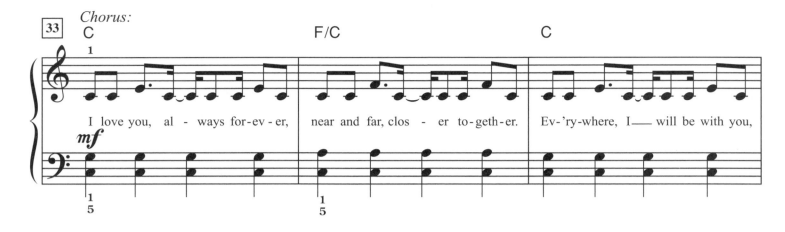

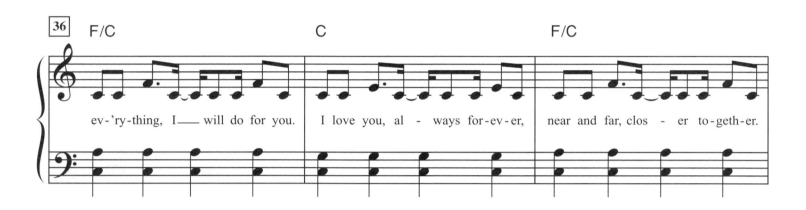

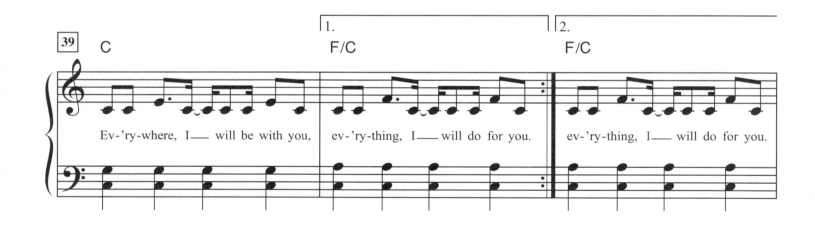

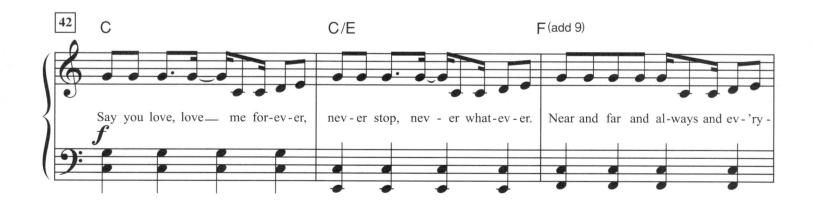

Verse 3:
You've got the most unbelievable blue eyes I've ever seen.
You've got me almost melting away as we lay there
Under blue sky with pure white stars,
Exotic sweetness, a magical time.
(To Chorus:)

I SWEAR

"I Swear" was a big hit ballad for two acts in 1994. It was a #1 song on the U.S. Hot Country Songs chart for John Michael Montgomery and was included on his album *Kickin' It Up*. The R & B male vocal quartet All-4-One also recorded the song, releasing it on their self-titled debut album. Their version climbed to #1 on the Billboard Hot 100 and stayed there for 11 weeks.

Words and Music by
Gary Baker and Frank Myers
Arranged by Dan Coates

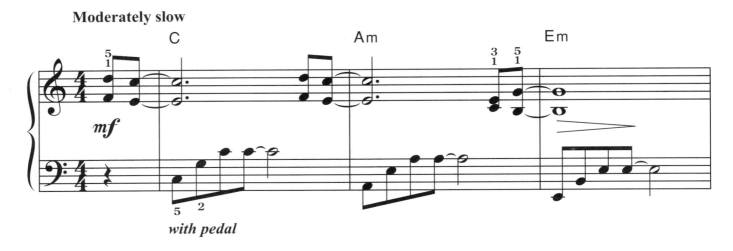

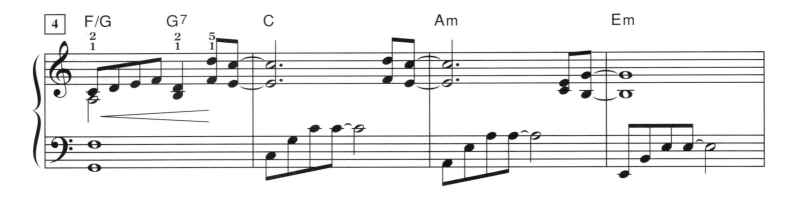

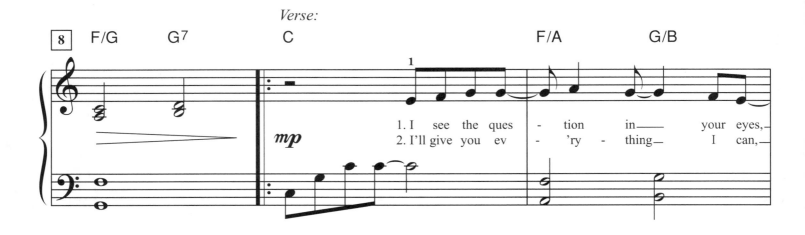

I HAVE NOTHING

Whitney Houston had a string of successful singles on the 1992 *The Bodyguard* soundtrack—the best-selling soundtrack of all time. The singles included "I Will Always Love You" (the most successful cover song of all time), "I'm Every Woman," "Run to You," "Queen of the Night," and "I Have Nothing." The soundtrack won a Grammy for Album of the Year and is 17 times platinum.

Words and Music by
Linda Thompson and David Foster
Arranged by Dan Coates

64

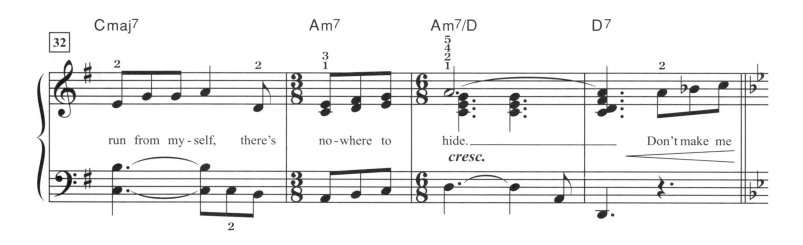

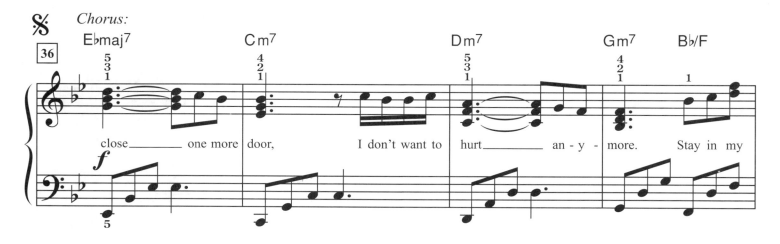

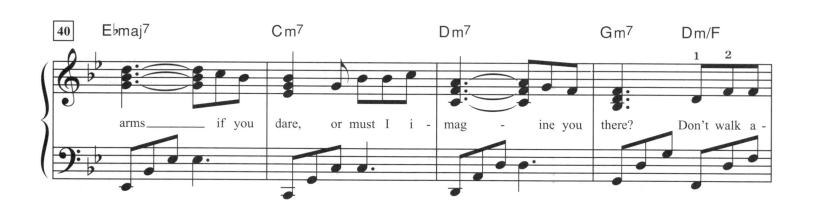

65

Don't walk a - way from me.____ Don't you dare walk a -

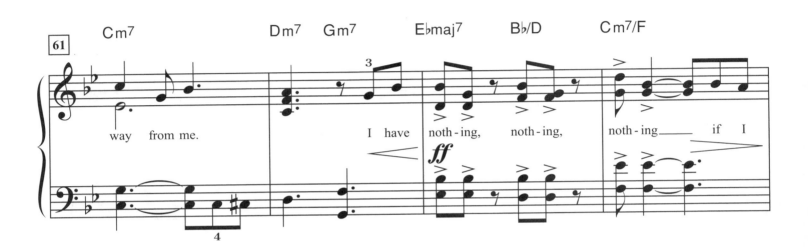

way from me. I have noth - ing, noth - ing, noth - ing____ if I

don't have you.

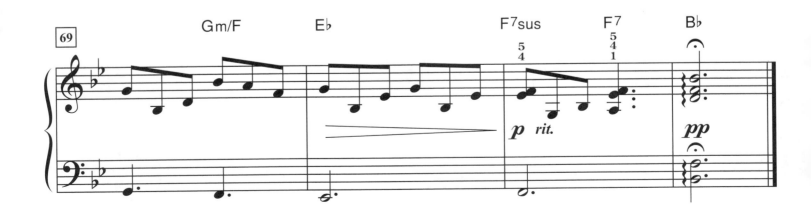

I'LL BE THERE FOR YOU
(Theme from *Friends*)

"I'll Be There for You" is the theme song from the popular sitcom *Friends* and was recorded in 1994 by the powerpop band The Rembrandts. Over its 10-year run on NBC (1994–2004), *Friends* won 6 Emmy Awards, 2 Golden Globe Awards, 12 People's Choice Awards, and 2 Screen Actors Guild Awards. The show both reflected and shaped young urban culture at the end of the 20th century—in fashion, speech, and lifestyle.

Music by Michael Skloff
Words by David Crane, Marta Kauffman,
Allee Willis, Phil Solem, Danny Wilde
Arranged by Dan Coates

1. So, no___ one told you life___ was gon - na be___ this way.
2. You're still___ in bed at ten___ and work be - gan___ at eight.

Your job's___ a joke, you're broke,___ your love life's D. O. A.
You've burned___ your break - fast, so___ far, ev - 'ry - thing is great.

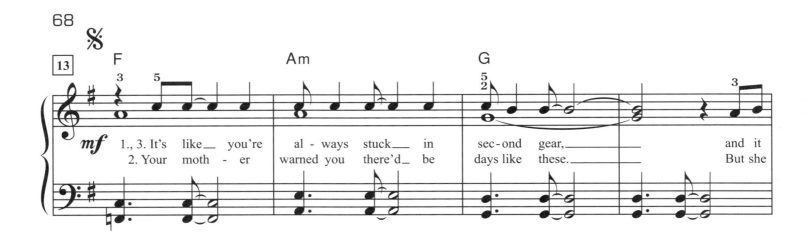

13

F / **Am** / **G**

mf

1., 3. It's like__ you're al - ways stuck__ in sec - ond gear,_____ and it
2. Your moth - er warned you there'd_ be days like these._____ But she

17

F / **C** / **Dsus** / **D**

has-n't been__ your day, your week,__ your month, or e - ven your year. But
did-n't tell__ you when the world_ has brought you down to your knees, that

cresc. poco a poco

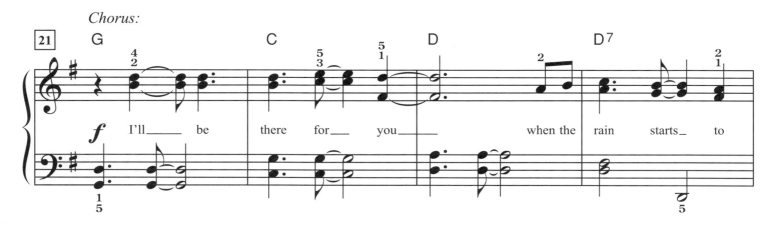

Chorus:

21

G / **C** / **D** / **D7**

f I'll____ be there for__ you____ when the rain starts_ to

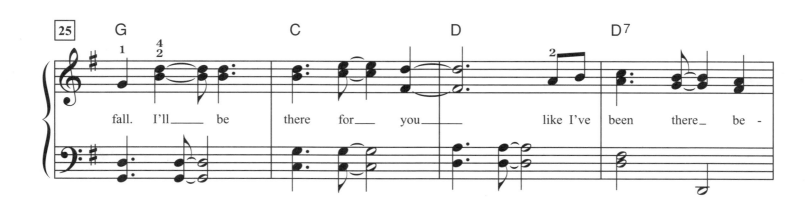

25

G / **C** / **D** / **D7**

fall. I'll____ be there for__ you____ like I've been there_ be -

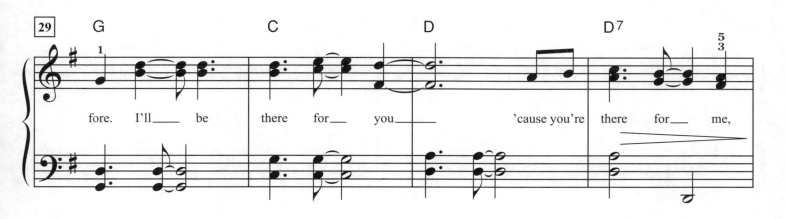

fore. I'll____ be there for____ you____ 'cause you're there for____ me,

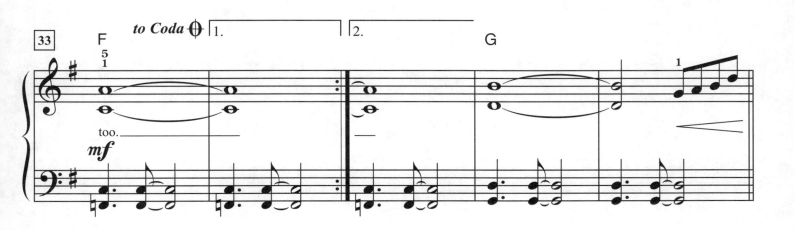

to Coda ⊕ |1. |2. G

too.____

mf

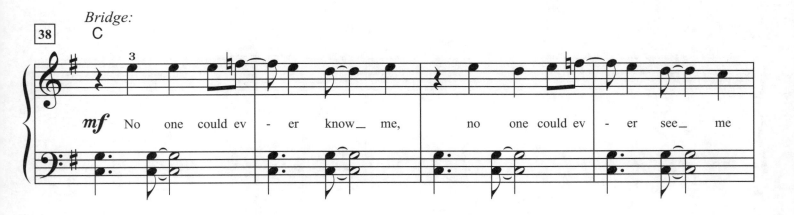

Bridge:
C

mf No one could ev - er know__ me, no one could ev - er see__ me

Em

since you're the on - ly one__ who knows what it's like to be__ me.

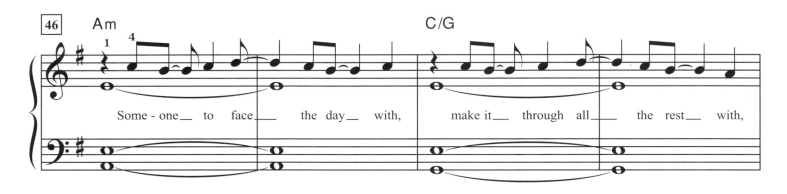

Some - one__ to face__ the day__ with, make it__ through all__ the rest__ with,

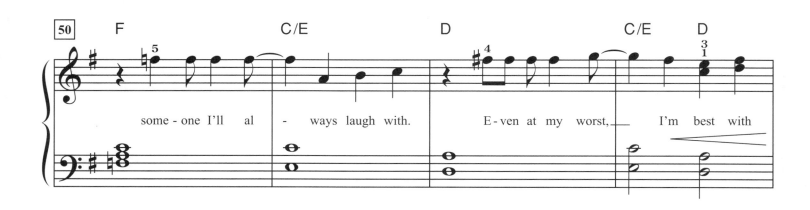

some - one I'll al - ways laugh with. E - ven at my worst,__ I'm best with

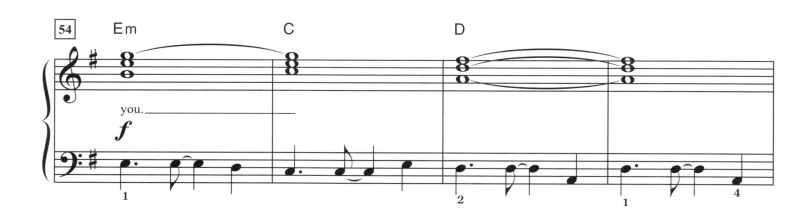

you._____

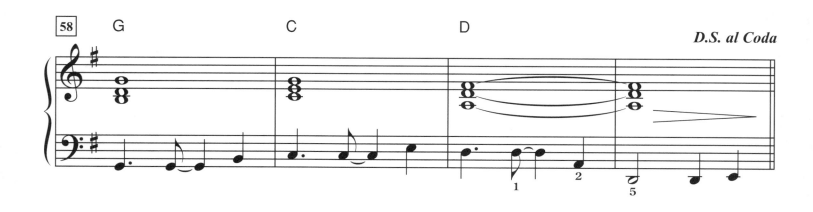

D.S. al Coda

Coda

G   C   D

I'll____ be there for__ you____ when the

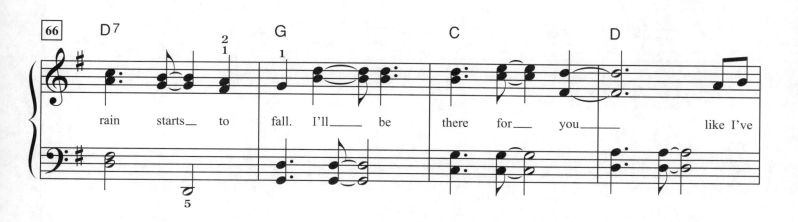

66 D7   G   C   D

rain starts__ to fall. I'll____ be there for__ you____ like I've

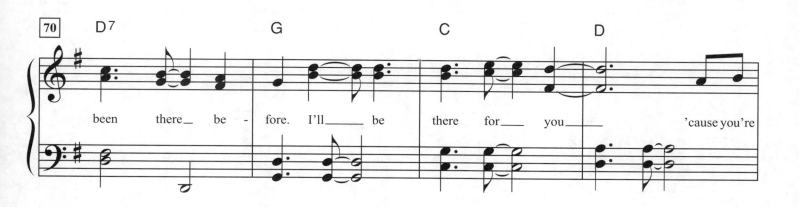

70 D7   G   C   D

been there__ be - fore. I'll____ be there for__ you____ 'cause you're

74 D7   F   G

there for__ me, too._____ *rit. e dim.*   *mf*

LIVIN' LA VIDA LOCA

"Livin' la Vida Loca" (Living the Crazy Life) is from Puerto Rican pop singer Ricky Martin's 1999 self-titled album, which contained material from Desmond Child, William Orbit, Robi Draco Rosa and Diane Warren, and guest performances by Madonna and Turkish singer Sertab Erener. The album was certified seven times platinum and sold over 17 million copies worldwide. "Livin' la Vida Loca" reached the top of the Billboard Hot 100 and held that position for five weeks.

Words and Music by
Robi Rosa and Desmond Child
Arranged by Dan Coates

14

17 Cm

mf 2. She's in - to new sen - sa - tions,
3. *See additional lyrics*

19 new kicks in the can - dle - light.__ She's got a

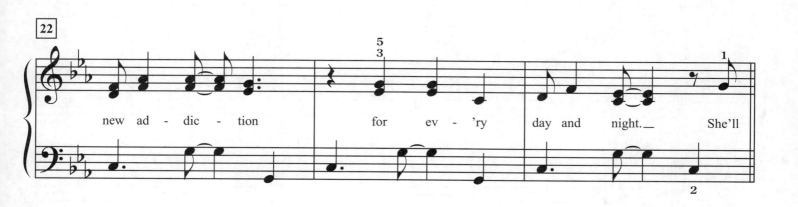

22 new ad - dic - tion for ev - 'ry day and night.__ She'll

74

56
1.
2.
D.S. al Coda
She'll
Coda
Cm
B♭
Up - side, in - side out, she's liv - in' la vi - da lo -
63
Cm
- ca. She'll push and pull you down,
66
B♭
Cm
liv - in' la vi - da lo - ca. Her lips are dev -
69
B♭
Cm
- il red and her skin's the col - or of mo - cha.

She will___ wear___ you out, li - vin' la vi - da lo -

- ca, liv - in' la vi - da lo - ca.

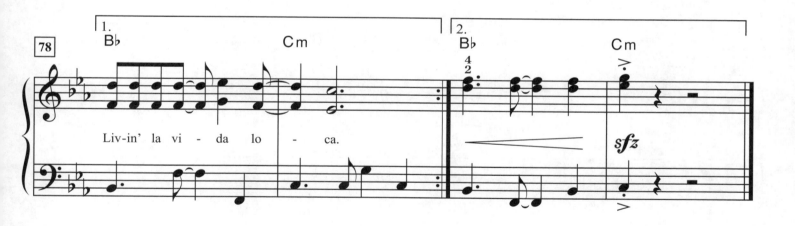

1. Liv-in' la vi - da lo - ca. 2.

Verse 3:
Woke up in New York City
In a funky, cheap hotel.
She took my heart and she took my money.
She must've slipped me a sleeping pill.

She never drinks the water
And makes you order French champagne.
Once you've had a taste of her,
You'll never be the same.
Yeah, she'll make you go insane.
(To Chorus:)

LOVE IS

Vanessa Williams has had a very successful career in the entertainment industry beginning with being the first African American Miss America, then a professional singer and actress. Brian McKnight has also had great success as a 16 time Grammy nominee, songwriter, arranger, producer, pop and R & B musician, radio personality, and Broadway star. Together they recorded "Love Is" (1993) which appeared on the *Beverly Hills 90210* soundtrack and was nominated for a Grammy for Best Pop Collaboration with Vocals.

Words and Music by
John Keller, Tonio K. and Michael Caruso
Arranged by Dan Coates

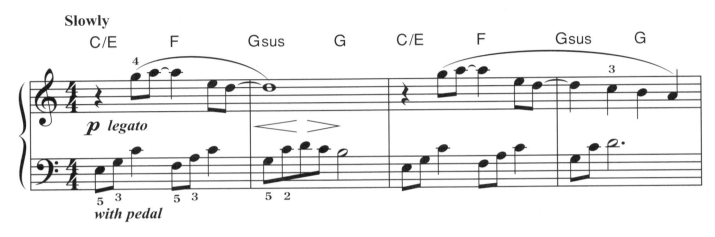

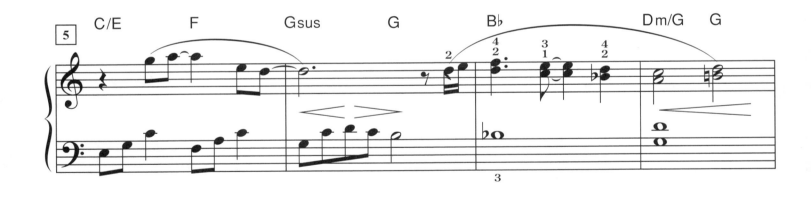

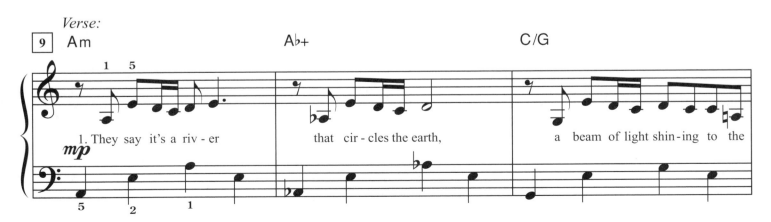

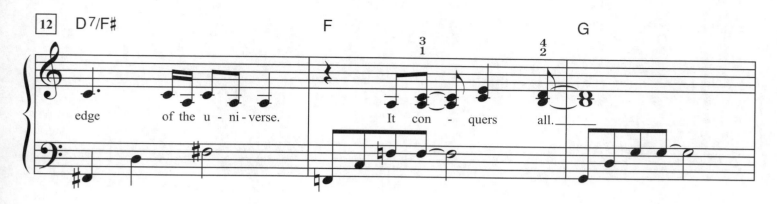

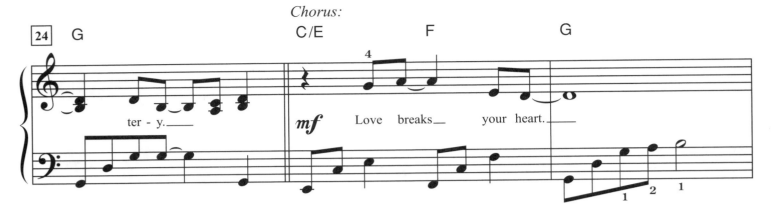

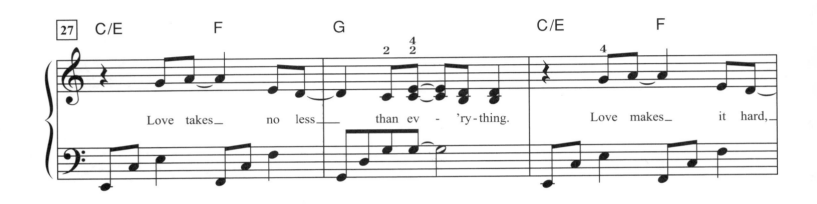

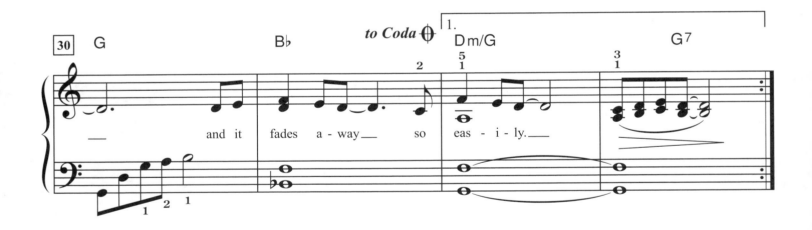

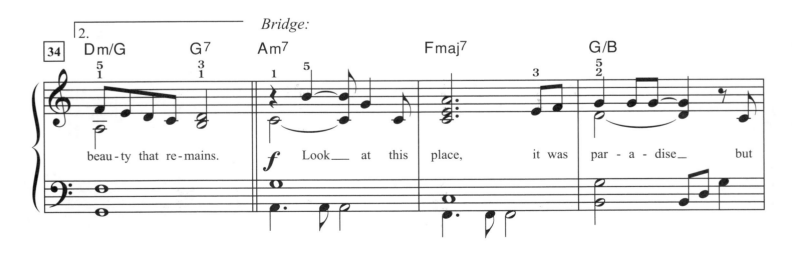

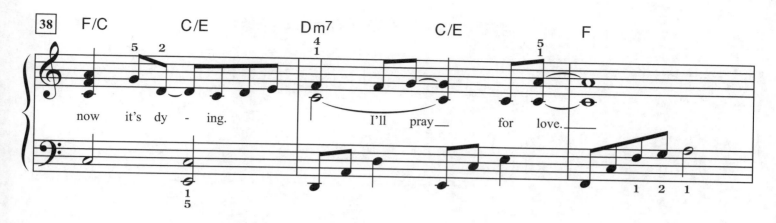

38   F/C   C/E   Dm7   C/E   F

now it's dy - ing.   I'll pray__ for love.__

41   Dm7   C/E   G   *D.S. al Coda*

I'll take__ my chanc - es that it's not too__ late.__

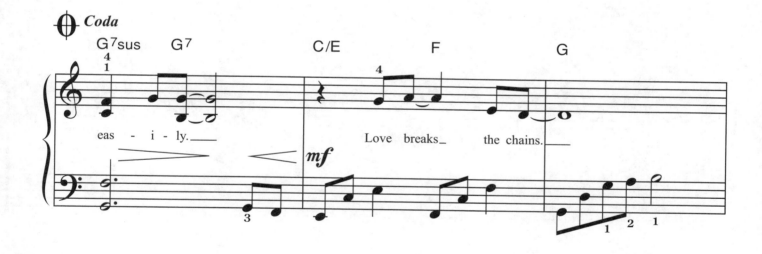

Coda

G7sus   G7   C/E   F   G

eas - i - ly.__   Love breaks__ the chains.__   *mf*

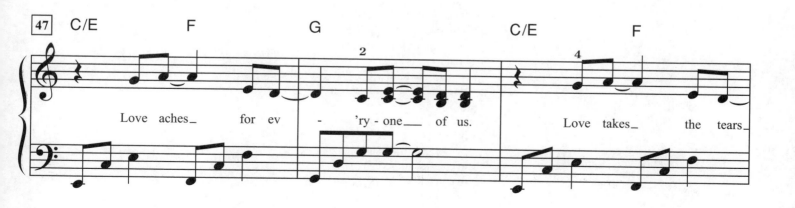

47   C/E   F   G   C/E   F

Love aches__ for ev - 'ry - one__ of us.   Love takes__ the tears__

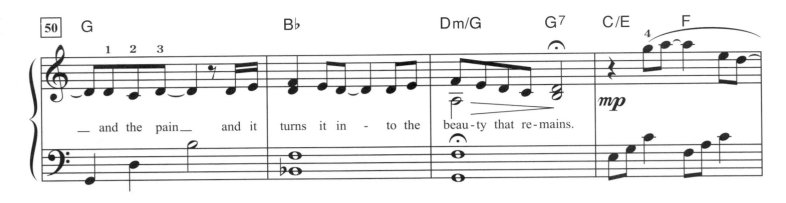

and the pain___ and it turns it in - to the beau-ty that re-mains.

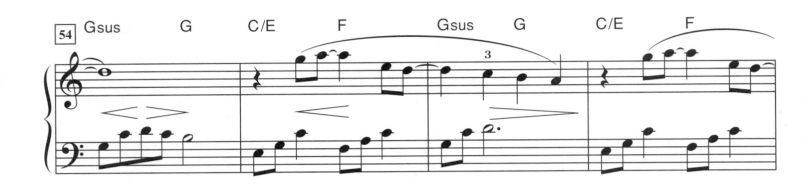

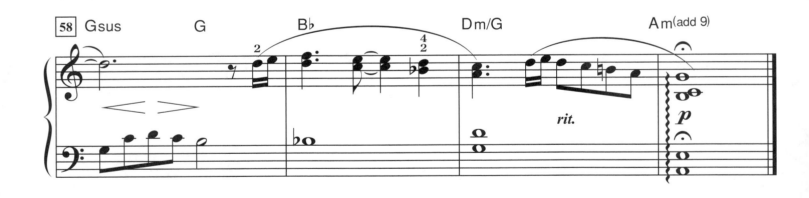

Verse 3:
In this world we've created,
In this place that we live,
In the blink of an eye, babe,
The darkness slips in.
Love lights the world,
Unites the lovers for eternity.
(To Chorus 2:)

Chorus 2:
Love breaks the chains.
Love aches for every one of us.
Love takes the tears and the pain
And it turns it into
The beauty that remains.
(To Bridge:)

LOVE WILL LEAD YOU BACK

"Love Will Lead You Back" is the second single from New York native Taylor Dayne's second album *Can't Fight Fate* (1990). Dayne's international success began with the release of her hit "Tell It to My Heart" (1988) which established her as an electrifying performer of up-tempo, dance music.

Words and Music by Diane Warren
Arranged by Dan Coates

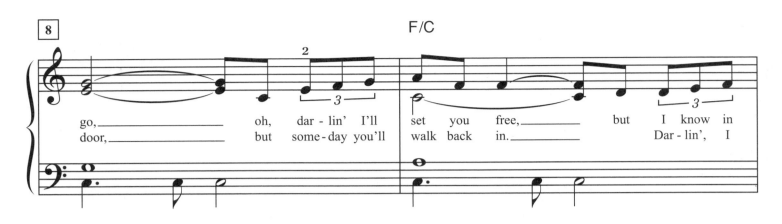

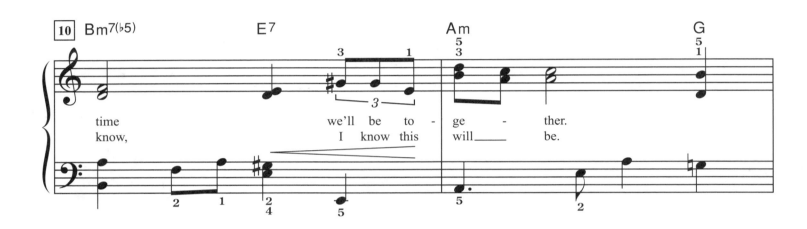

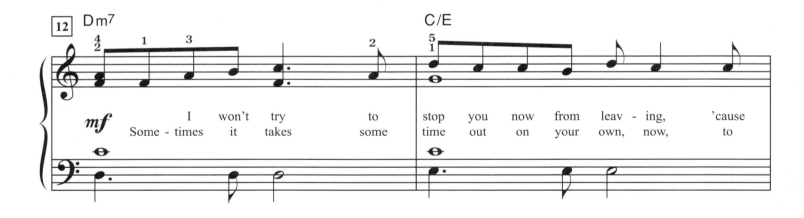

Chorus:

back, some-day I just know___ that love will lead you

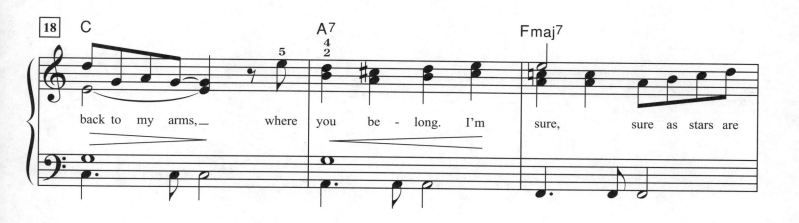

back to my arms,___ where you be - long. I'm sure, sure as stars are

shin - ing, one day you will find me a - gain,___ it won't be long.___ One of these

dim.

days, oh, love will lead you back.___ 2. One of these

Bridge:

back. _____

mp

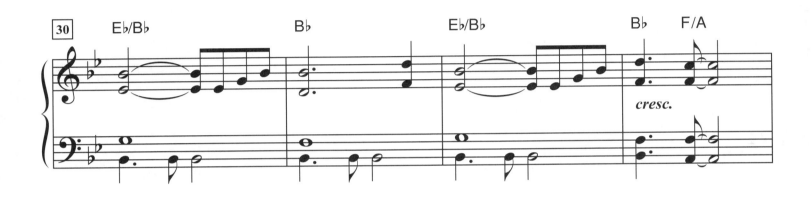

cresc.

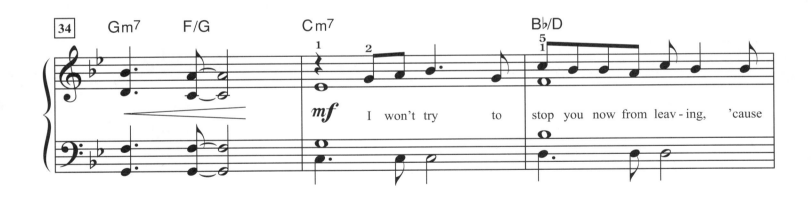

mf I won't try to stop you now from leav-ing, 'cause

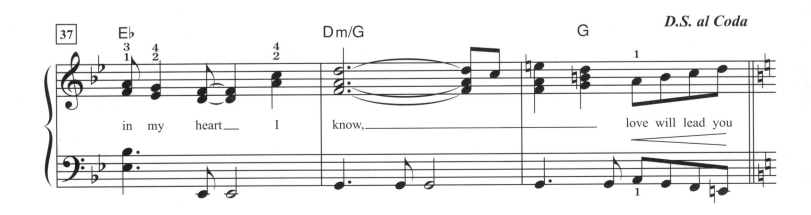

D.S. al Coda

in my heart ___ I know, _____ love will lead you

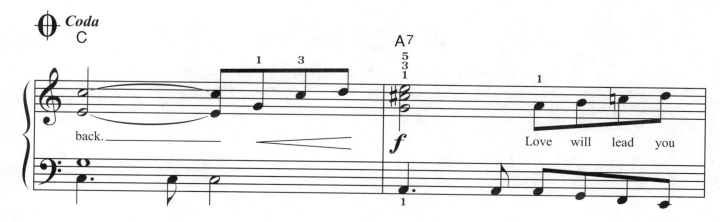

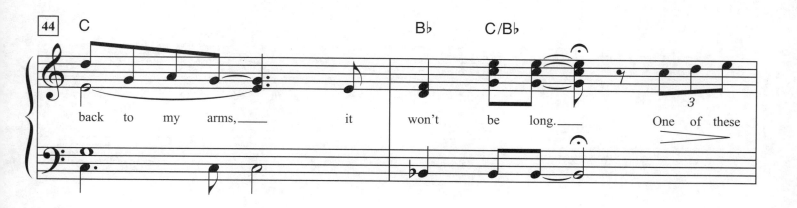

MACARENA

In 2002 VH1 aired "100 Greatest One Hit Wonders." "Macarena" was the #1 greatest one hit wonder. Originally released in 1995 by the Spanish duo Los del Río, the song was remixed by The Bayside Boys and became a summer hit in 1996, holding the #1 spot on the Billboard Hot 100 for 14 weeks—one of the longest #1 runs in history. At the 1996 nationally-televised Democratic National Convention in Chicago, the convention delegates performed the Macarena dance as they waited for the speakers. The dance was taught to them by a Wisconsin delegate who learned the dance from her 12-year-old daughter who learned the dance in Spanish class.

Words and Music by
Antonio Romero and Rafael Ruiz
Arranged by Dan Coates

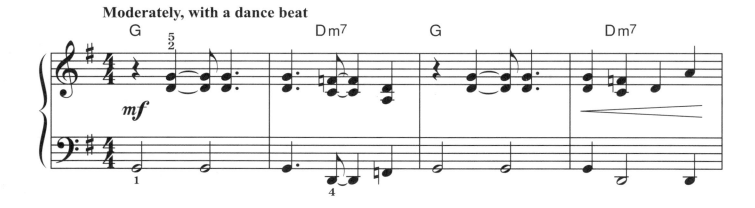

ONE OF US

Joan Osborne released "One of Us" in 1995 on her debut album *Relish*. The song, although controversial (it was criticized by the Catholic League), was popular and climbed to #4 on the Billboard Hot 100. Osborne's popularity continued with her participation in the Lilith Fair (1997–99), a concert tour created by Canadian singer/songwriter Sarah McLachlan to promote female solo artists and female-led bands.

Words and Music by Eric Bazilian
Arranged by Dan Coates

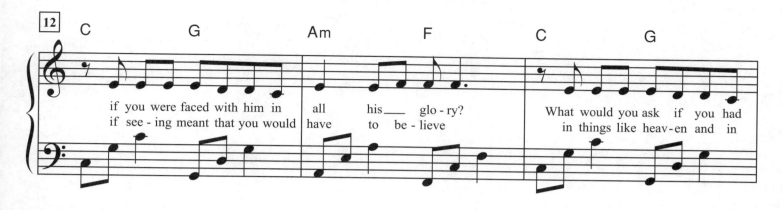

12 C   G   Am   F   C   G

if you were faced with him in all his___ glo - ry?
if see - ing meant that you would have to be - lieve

What would you ask if you had
in things like heav-en and in

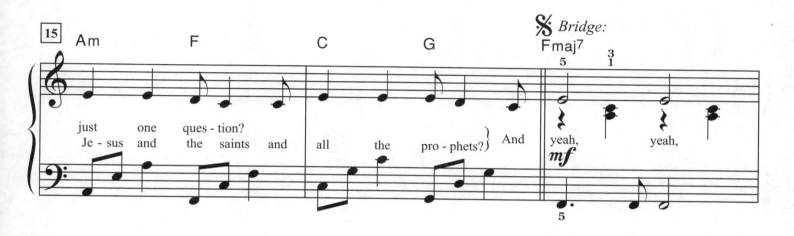

15 Am   F   C   G   *Bridge:* Fmaj⁷

just one ques - tion?
Je - sus and the saints and all the pro - phets? And

yeah, yeah,

mf

18 G   Fmaj⁷   G

God is___ great. Yeah, yeah, God is___ good.

21 Fmaj⁷   G   *Chorus:* Am   F

Yeah, yeah, yeah, yeah, yeah. What if God was one of us?___

cresc.   *f*

94

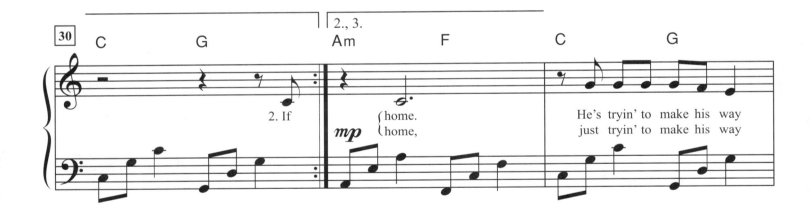

THE PRAYER

"The Prayer" was recorded by Canadian superstar Céline Dion and Italian tenor Andrea Bocelli in 1998, both as a duet and as solo performances. It was on the *Quest for Camelot* soundtrack, won a Golden Globe award for Best Original Song, and was also nominated for an Academy Award. The song was also covered in 2004 by *Australian Idol* runner up Anthony Callea and quickly became the fastest-selling single to be released by an Australian artist.

Words and Music by
Carole Bayer Sager and David Foster
Italian Lyric by Alberto Testa and Tony Renis
Arranged by Dan Coates

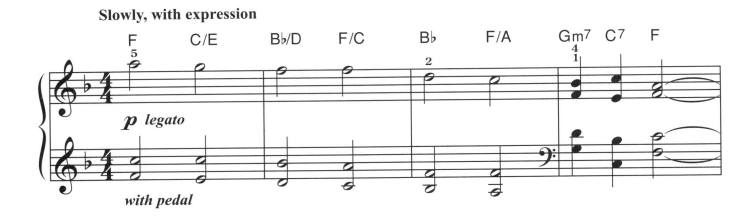

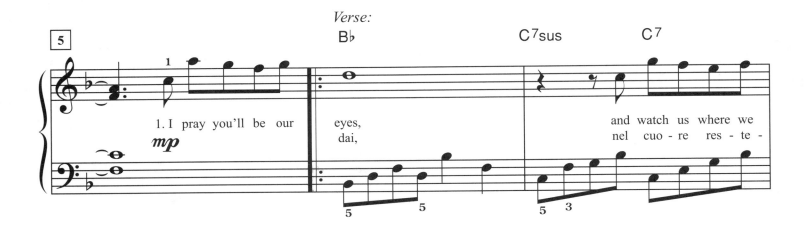

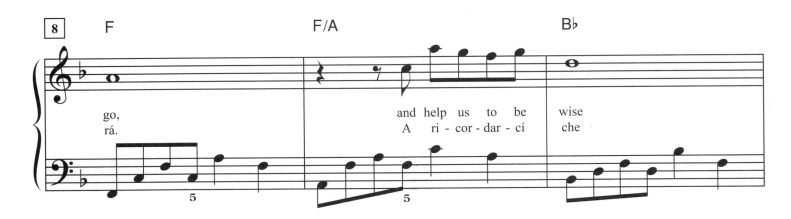

97

98

Bridge:

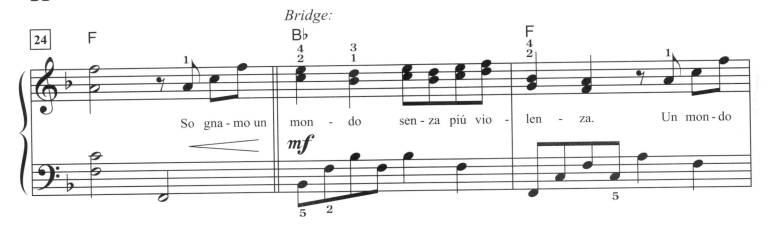

So gna - mo un mon - do sen - za piú vio - len - za. Un mon - do

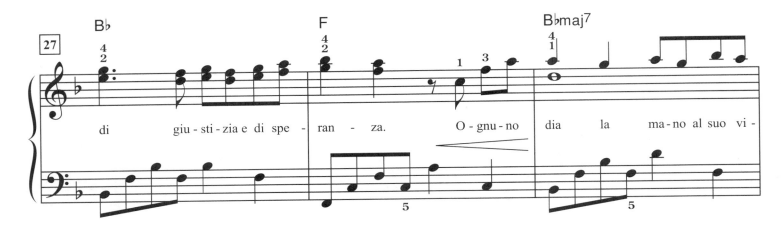

di giu - sti - zia e di spe - ran - za. O - gnu - no dia la ma - no al suo vi -

ci - no sim - bo - lo di pa - ce, di fra - ter - ni - tá.

Verse:

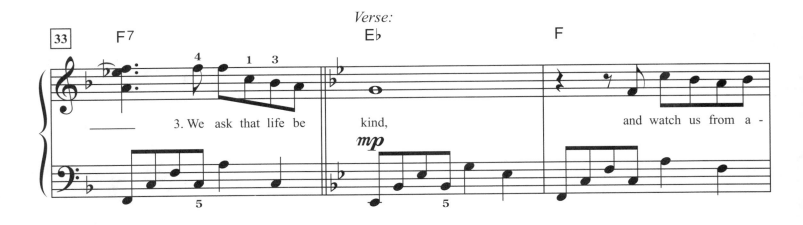

3. We ask that life be kind, and watch us from a -

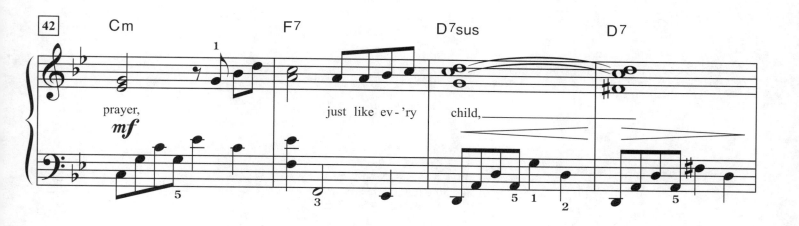

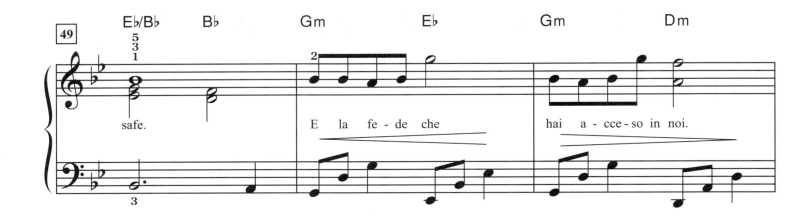

Verse 2 (English lyric):
I pray we'll find your light,
And hold it in our hearts
When stars go out each night.
Let this be our prayer,
When shadows fill our day.
Lead us to a place,
Guide us with your grace.
Give us faith so we'll be safe.

Verse 3 (Italian lyric):
La forza che ci dai
é il desiderio che.
Ognuno trovi amore
Intorno e dentro sé.

BECAUSE YOU LOVED ME

Céline Dion recorded "Because You Loved Me" for the 1996 film *Up Close & Personal*, a romance/drama inspired by the story of Jessica Savitch, the first female news anchor on television. The song was a huge hit, winning a Grammy Award, and was nominated for an Academy Award and Golden Globe Award.

Words and Music by Diane Warren
Arranged by Dan Coates

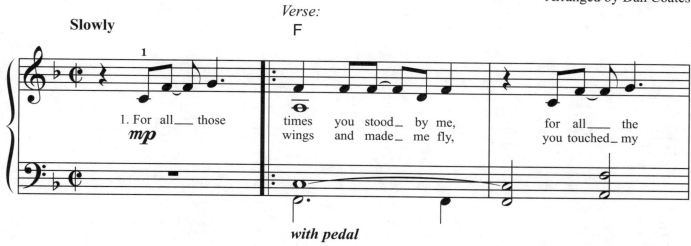

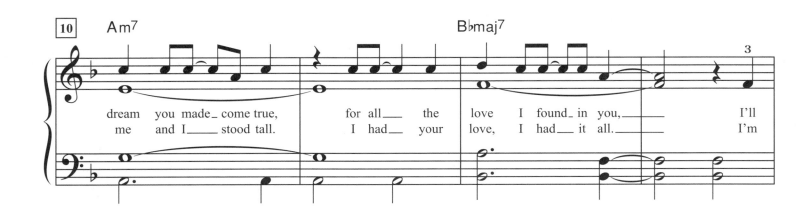

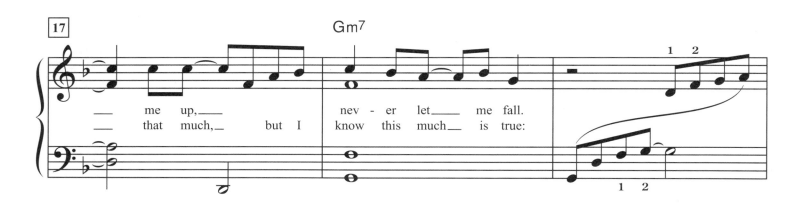

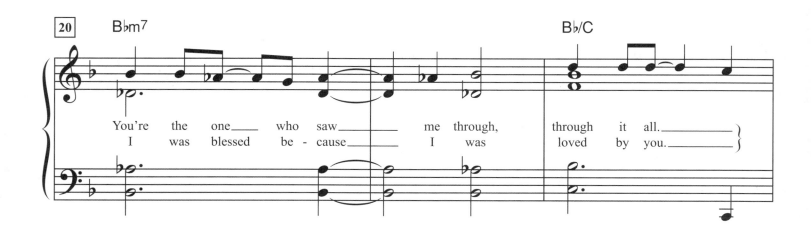

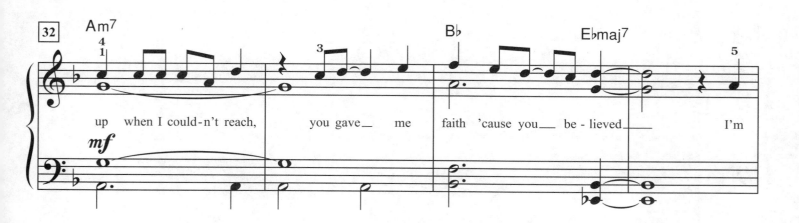

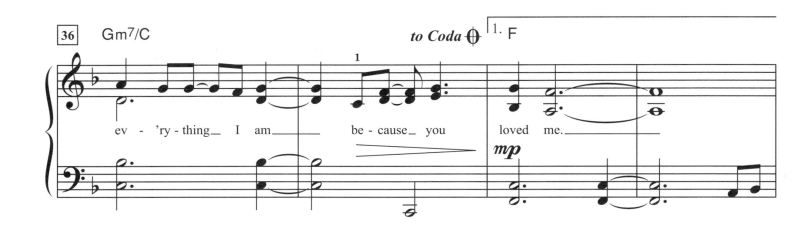

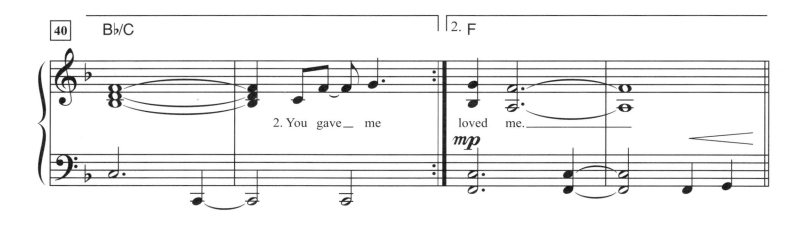

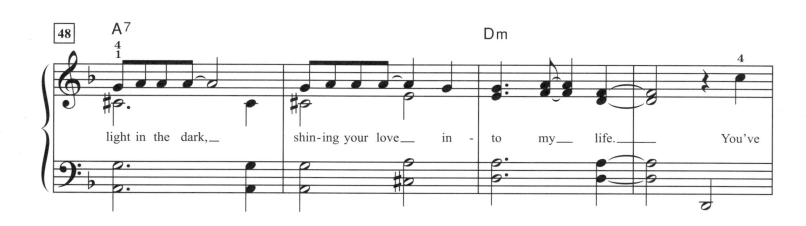

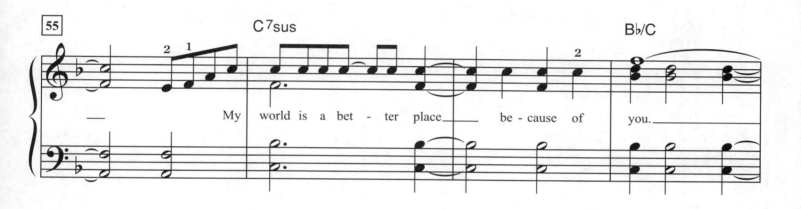

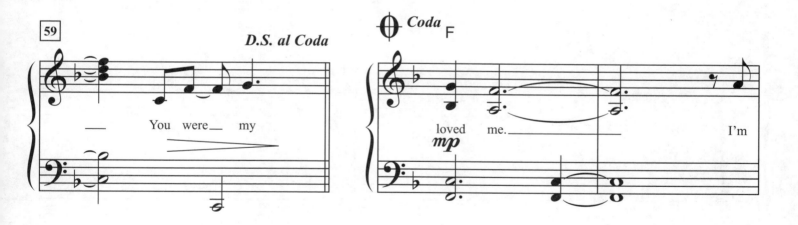

THE RIVER

Garth Brooks is one of the most successful artists in country and pop music history with over 70 hit singles, 15 charted albums, and over 123 million albums sold in the Unites States alone. Brooks was influenced by a wide range of singers—from George Strait to James Taylor to Bruce Springsteen—and was influential in opening up country music to a wider audience than ever before. "The River" is from his third album, *Ropin' the Wind* (1991), which had advanced orders of 4 million copies and debuted at #1 on both the pop and country charts when released.

Words and Music by
Victoria Shaw and Garth Brooks
Arranged by Dan Coates

Chorus:

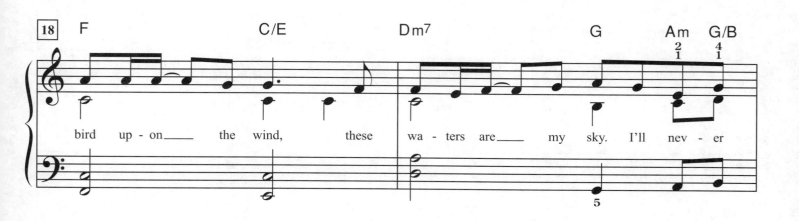

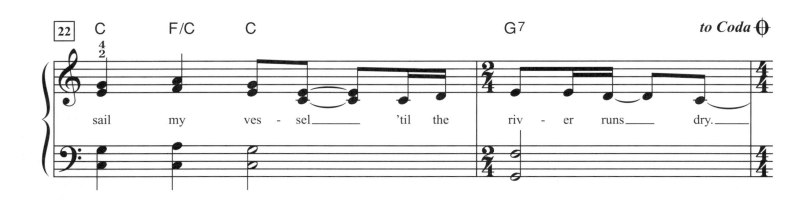

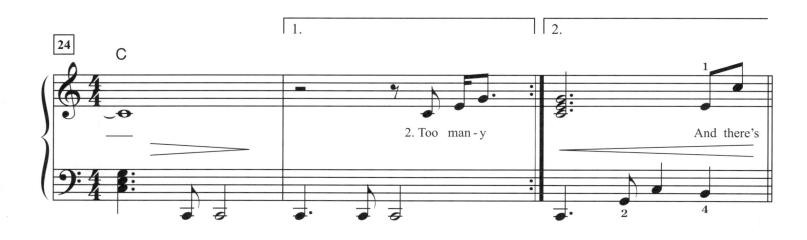

Verse 2:
Too many times we stand aside
And let the waters slip away
'Til what we put off 'til tomorrow
Has now become today.
So don't you sit upon the shoreline
And say you're satisfied.
Choose to chance the rapids
And dare to dance the tide.
Yes I will…
(To Chorus:)

SMOOTH

In 1999 "Smooth" from Santana's album *Supernatural* spent 12 weeks at the #1 spot on Billboard Hot 100 and won three Grammy Awards: Record of the Year, Song of the Year, and Best Pop Collaboration with Vocals. It featured the talent of Rob Thomas (lyrics/lead vocals), Carlos Santana (rock guitar), and Itaal Shur (songwriting).

Words and Music by
Itaal Shur and Rob Thomas
Arranged by Dan Coates

111

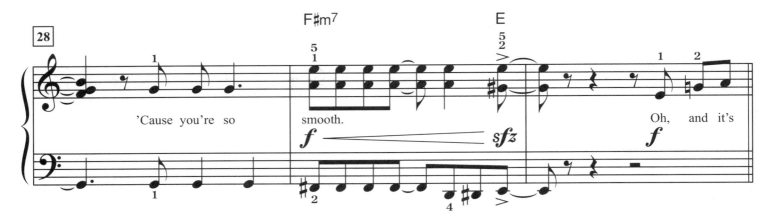

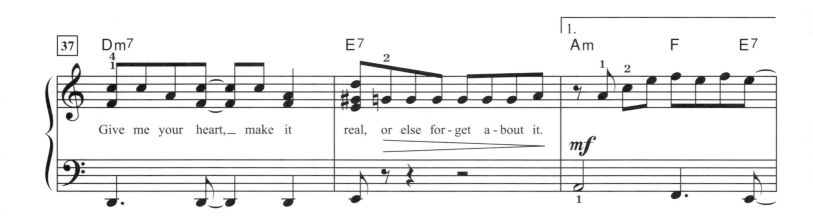

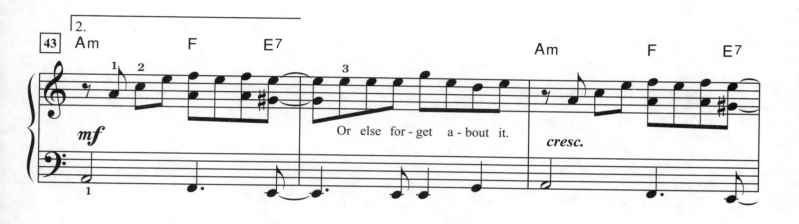

Verse 2:
Well, I'll tell you one thing,
If you should leave, it'd be a crying shame.
In every breath and every word
I hear your name calling me out, yeah.
Well, out from the barrio,
You hear my rhythm on your radio.
You feel the tugging of the world,
So soft and slow, turning you 'round and 'round.
And if you said this life ain't good enough,
I would give my world to lift you up.
I could change my life to better suit your mood.
'Cause you're so smooth.
(To Chorus:)

THIS KISS

"This Kiss" is the first single from country artist Faith Hill's third album *Faith* (1998). It reached #1 on the Billboard Country charts and became her breakthrough pop hit, establishing her as a successful crossover artist. Her fan base has remained strong over the last decade; Soul2Soul II, Hill's 2006 concert tour with husband Tim McGraw, became the top-grossing country concert tour of all time.

Words and Music by Robin Lerner,
Annie Roboff and Beth Nielsen Chapman
Arranged by Dan Coates

Moderately bright, in two

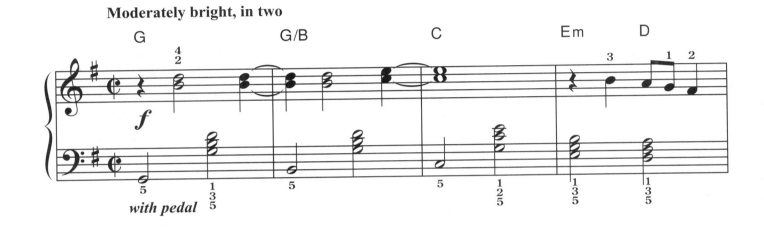

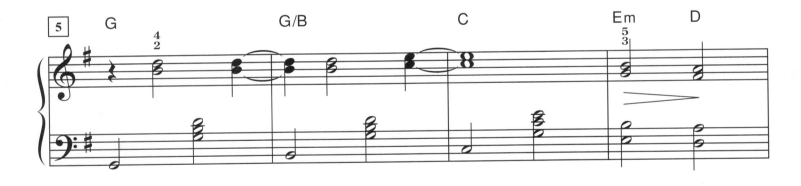

Verse:

1. I don't want an-oth-er heart-break. I don't need an-oth-er turn to cry,—
2. Cin-der-el-la said to Snow White, "How does love get so off course?"—

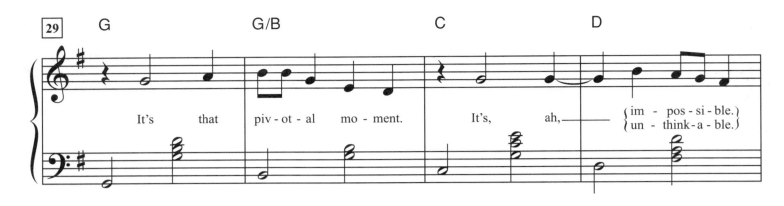

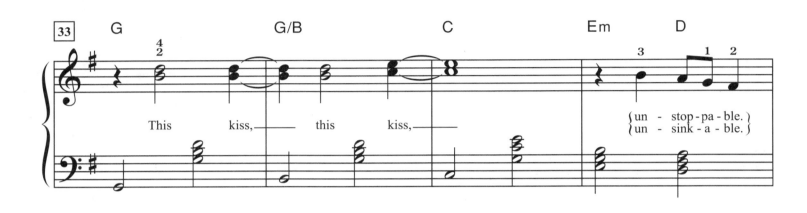

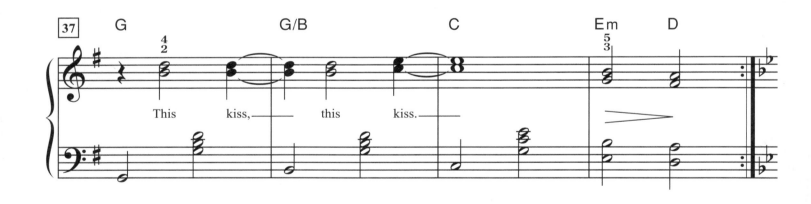

Bridge:

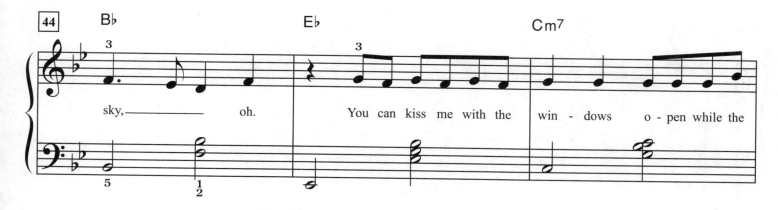

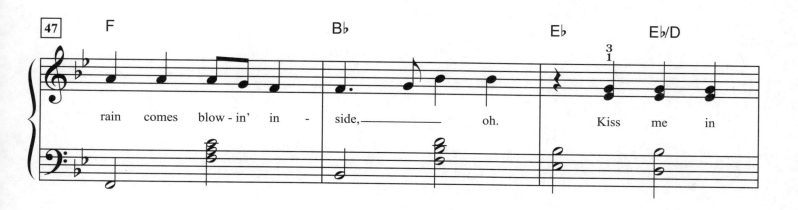

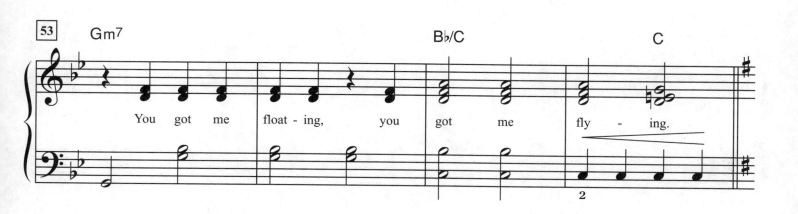

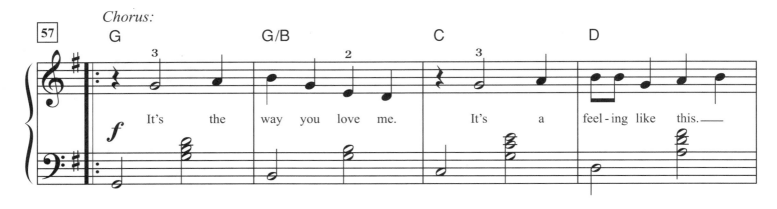

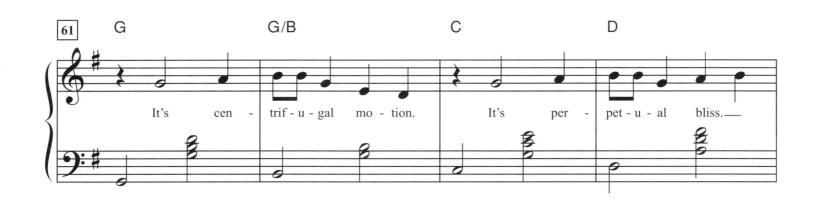

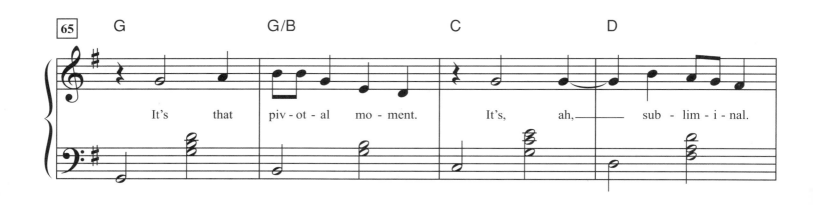

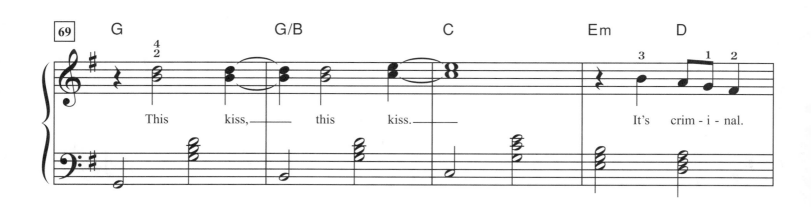

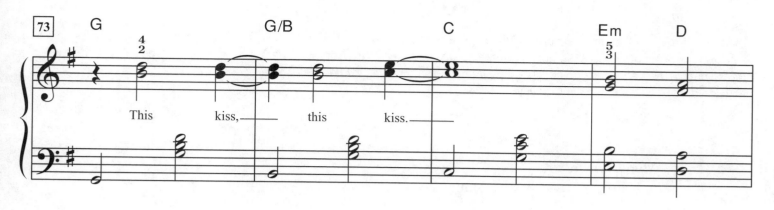

This kiss,___ this kiss.

It's the way you love me, ba - by.___

It's the way you love me, dar - ling.___

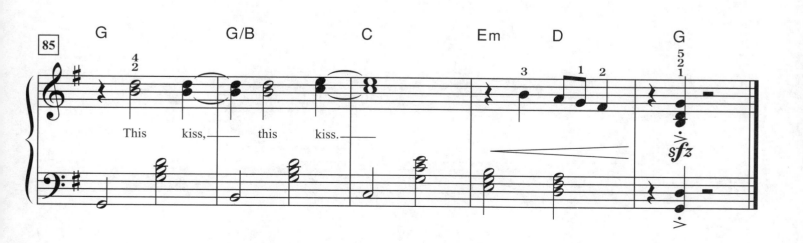

This kiss,___ this kiss.___

THANK YOU

"Thank You" was released in 1999 on English singer-songwriter Dido's debut album *No Angel* and reached a #3 chart position in the U.K. and United States. Rapper Eminem sampled the first few lines of "Thank You" and used it as the chorus for his critically acclaimed #1 single "Stan" (2000). He and Elton John performed a duet version live at the 2001 Grammy Awards, and Dido starred in the song's music video.

Words and Music by
Dido Armstrong and Paul Herman
Arranged by Dan Coates

Verse 2:
I drank too much last night, got bills to pay,
My head just feels in pain.
I missed the bus and there'll be hell today,
I'm late for work again.
And even if I'm there, they'll all imply
That I might not last the day.
And then you call me and it's not so bad, it's not so bad.
(To Chorus:)

UN-BREAK MY HEART

"Un-Break My Heart" is R & B singer Toni Braxton's second single from her second studio album *Secrets* (1996). She won a Grammy Award for the recording which topped the Billboard Hot 100 for 11 weeks. It would become her signature song and biggest hit of her career. She starred in the music video for the song with supermodel Tyson Beckford.

Words and Music by Diane Warren
Arranged by Dan Coates

Moderately slow

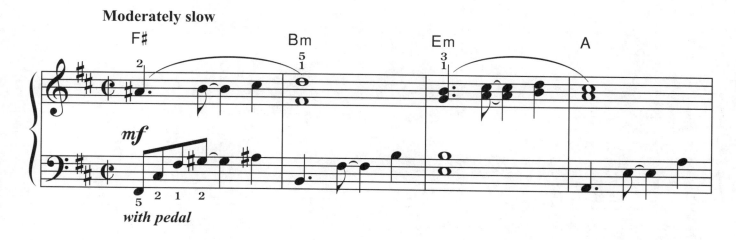

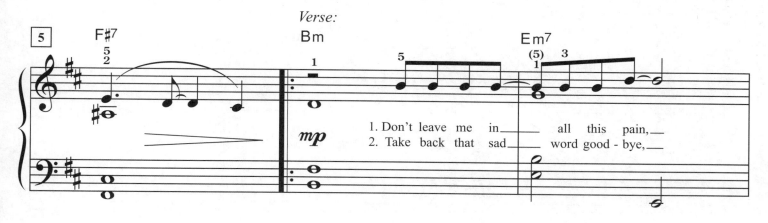

1. Don't leave me in ___ all this pain,
2. Take back that sad ___ word good - bye,

don't leave me out ___ in the rain. ___ Come back and bring
bring back the joy ___ to my life. ___ Don't leave me here

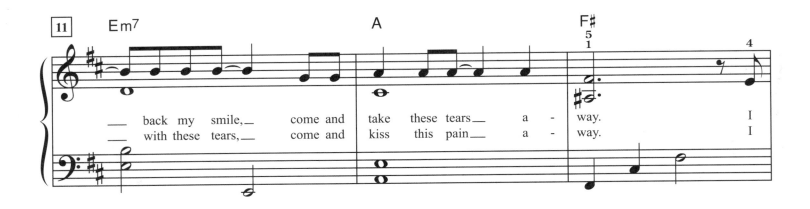

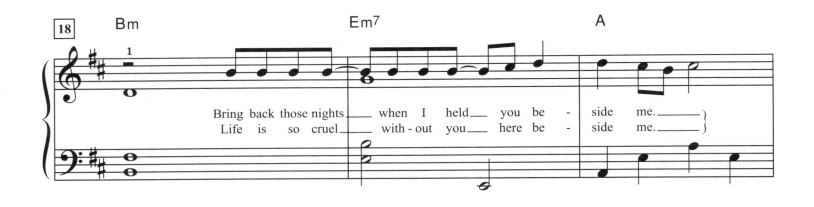

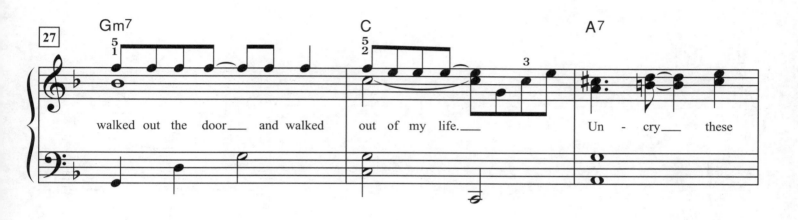

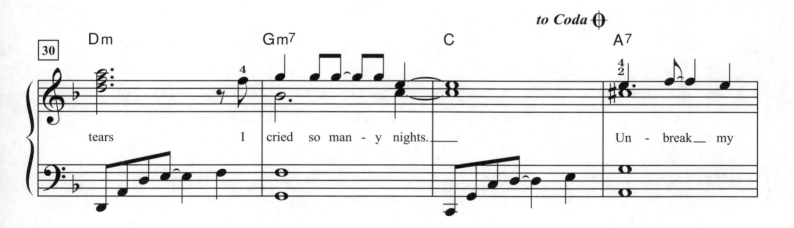

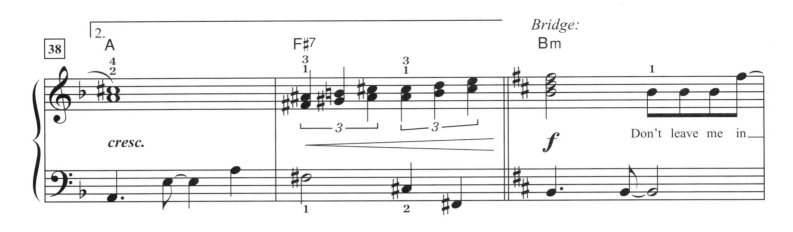

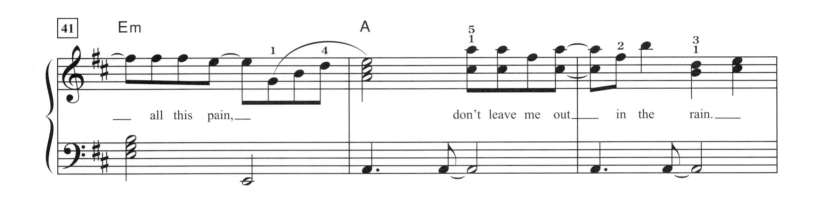

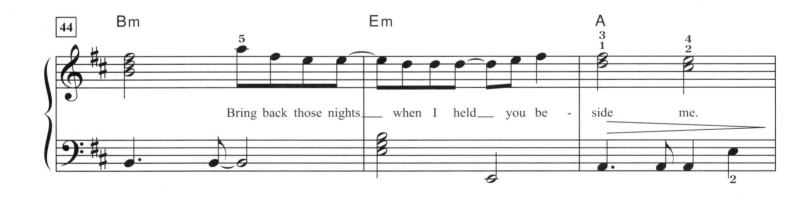

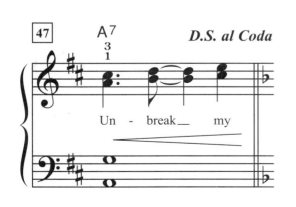

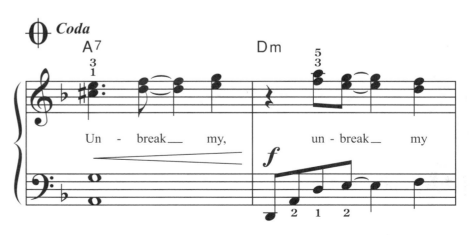

VALENTINE

Jim Brickman is a leading composer, performer, and recording artist in the world of adult contemporary music. His prolific career includes six gold and platinum albums, fifteen Top 10 Adult Contemporary radio hits, consistent #1 debuts on Billboard's New Age chart, and numerous awards and honors. He is the host of the weekly radio show *Your Weekend with Jim Brickman,* and has appeared on three televised PBS specials. His collaborations with artists include: Michael W. Smith, Kenny Loggins, Carly Simon, Herb Alpert, Collin Raye, Pam Tillis, Michael Bolton, Donny Osmond, Olivia Newton-John, and Martina McBride. "Valentine" was recorded with McBride in 1998.

Words and Music by
Jim Brickman and Jack Kugell
Arranged by Dan Coates

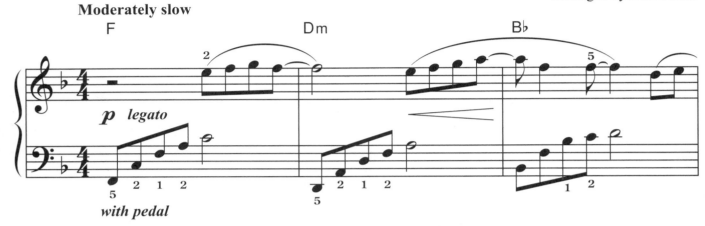

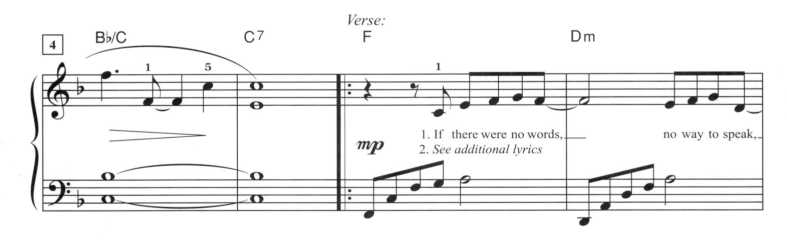

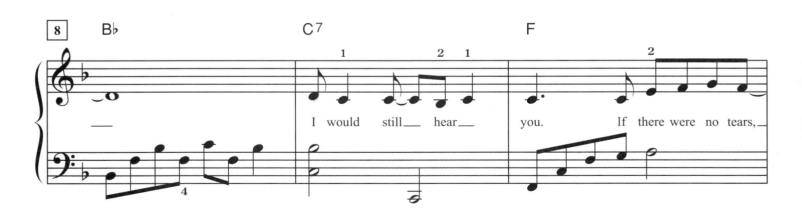

129

130

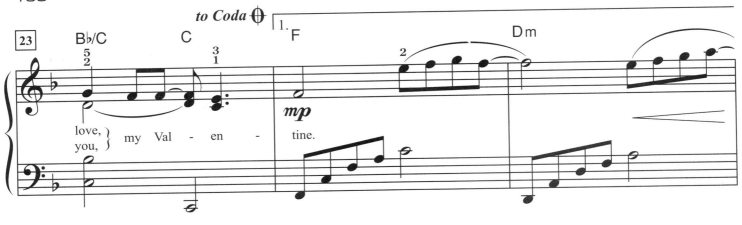

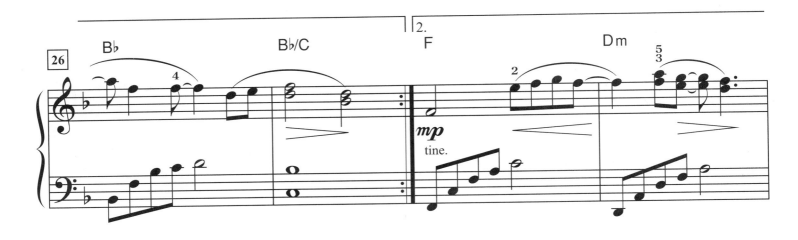

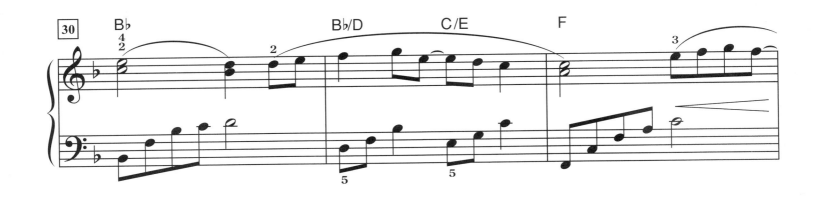

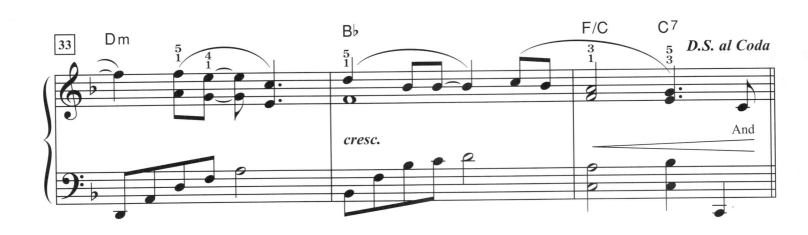

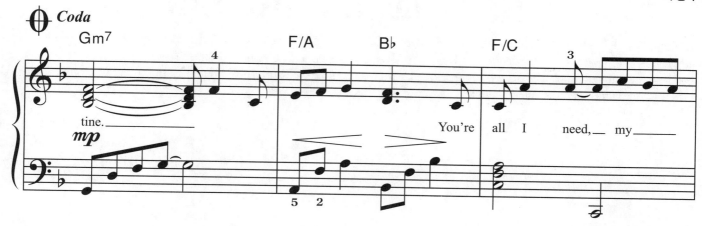

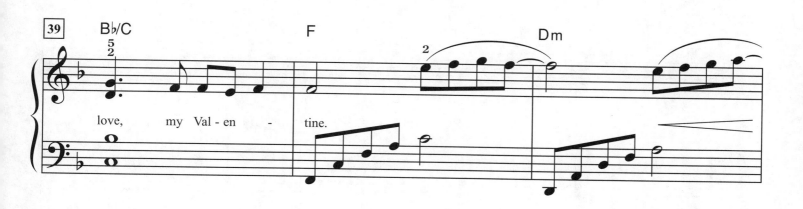

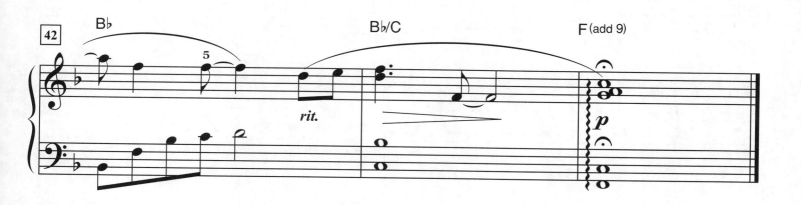

Verse 2:
All of my life,
I have been waiting for all you give to me.
You've opened my eyes
And shown me how to love unselfishly.
I've dreamed of this a thousand times before,
But in my dreams I couldn't love you more.
I will give you my heart until the end of time.
You're all I need, my love,
My Valentine.

WALKIN' ON THE SUN

The band Smash Mouth formed in 1994 in San Jose, California, and developed an eclectic sound, being known for recording numerous pop covers—songs from The Monkees, The Beatles, and The Four Seasons, to name a few—and drawing upon genres such as ska, surf, classic rock and punk. "Walkin' on the Sun" is from their double platinum debut album *Fush Yu Mang* (1997) and was their first major single.

Words and Music by
Steve Harwell, Gregory Camp,
Paul Delisle and Kevin Iannello
Arranged by Dan Coates

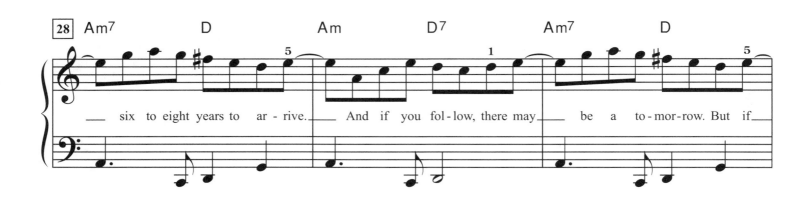

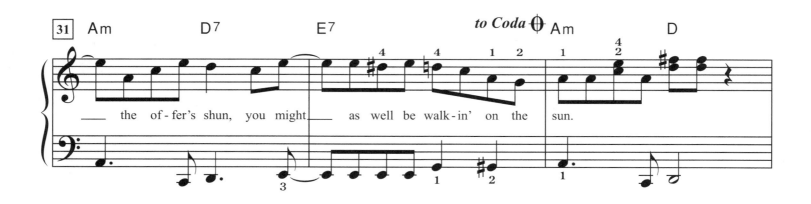

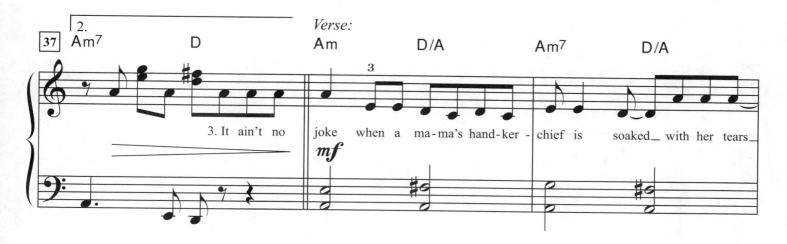

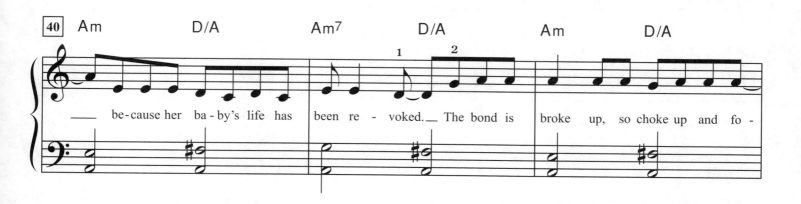

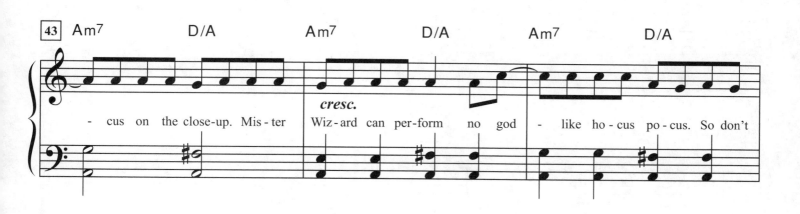

Verse 2:
Twenty-five years ago they spoke out
And they broke out of recession and oppression.
And together they toked and they folked out with guitars
Around a bonfire, just singin' and clappin', man, what the hell happened?
Yeah, some were spellbound, some were hell bound,
Some, they fell down and some got back up and fought back against the meltdown.
And their kids were hippie chicks, all hypocrites
Because their fashion is smashin' the true meaning of it.
(To Chorus:)

A WHOLE NEW WORLD
(from Walt Disney's *Aladdin*)

"A Whole New World" is the hit single from Walt Disney's animated feature *Aladdin* (1992). In the film it was sung by Brad (Caleb) Kane and Lea Salonga (the singing voices for Aladdin and Princess Jasmine) and during the closing credits by Peabo Bryson and Regina Belle. The ballad won the Academy Award for Best Original Song and became the only Disney song to hit #1 on the U.S. charts.

Words by Tim Rice
Music by Alan Menken
Arranged by Dan Coates

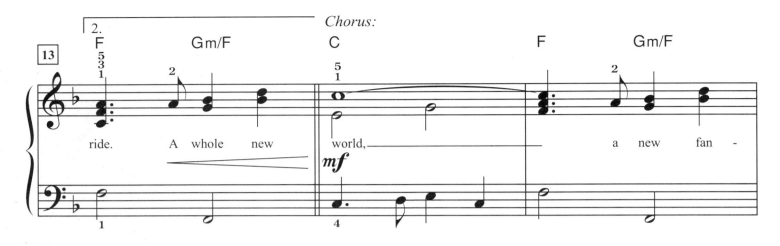

Chorus:

ride. A whole new   world,_____   a new fan -

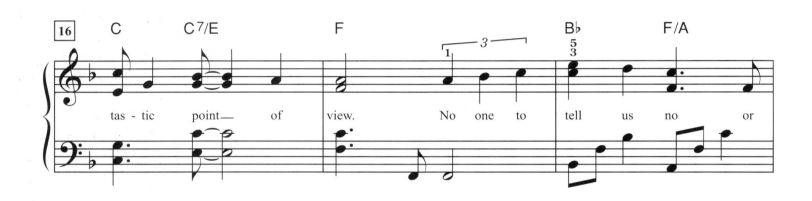

tas - tic point___ of view.   No one to tell us no or

where to go   or say we're on - ly dream - ing.   A whole new

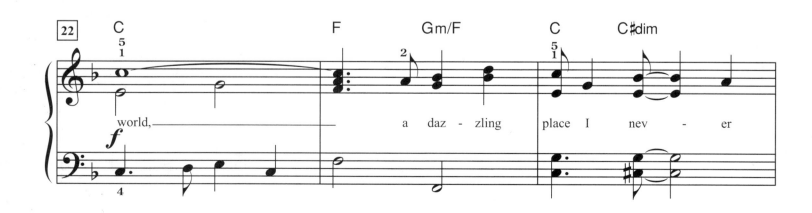

world,_____   a daz - zling place I nev - er

YOU'VE GOT A FRIEND IN ME
(from *Toy Story*)

Academy Award-winning songwriter, arranger, composer, singer and pianist Randy Newman wrote "You've Got a Friend in Me" for the 1995 Pixar film *Toy Story*. The movie won an Academy Special Achievement Award for being the first ever feature-length computer-animated film. Newman scored four other films for Pixar: *A Bugs Life*; *Cars*; *Monsters, Inc.*; and *Toy Story 2*.

Words and Music by Randy Newman
Arranged by Dan Coates

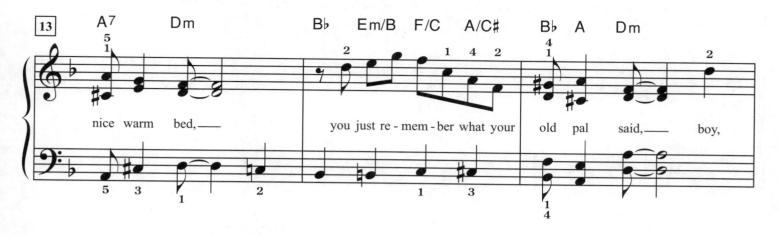

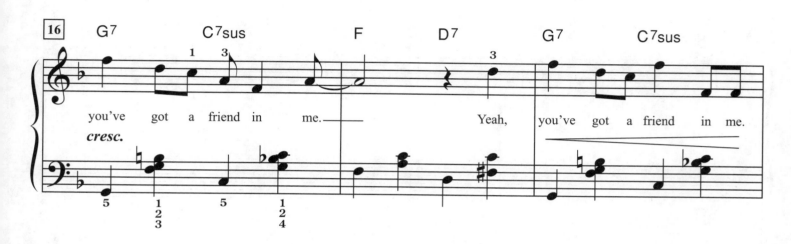

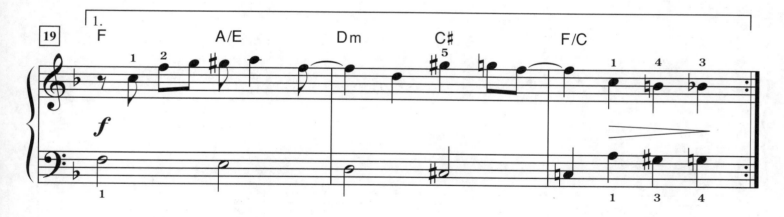

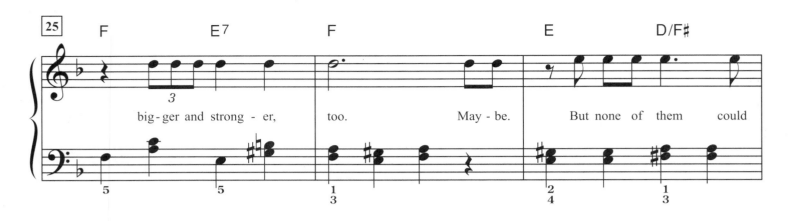

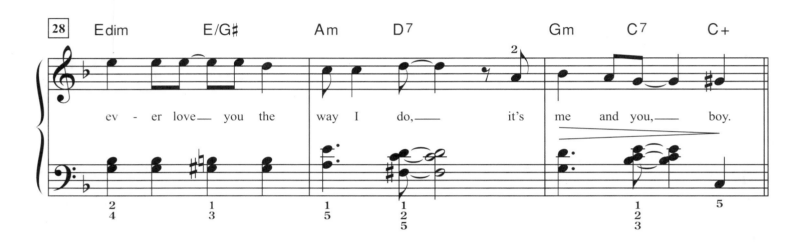

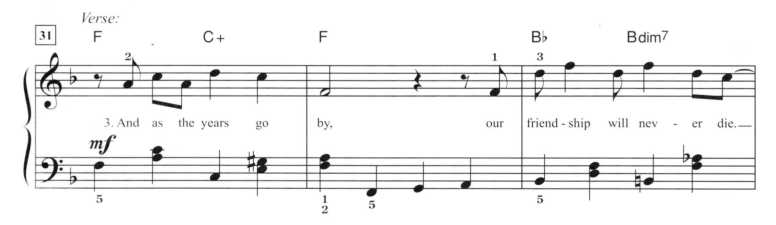